VT MILITES DICVNTVR

as soldiers are called

A Dictionary of Roman Military Terms and Terminology

M. C. Bishop

Per Lineam Valli 5

THE ARMATVRA PRESS

First published digitally in 2014 in Great Britain by The Armatura Press
Paperback edition 2014

ISBN 978-1-9102380-1-1

© 2014 M. C. Bishop

Design and layout by M. C. Bishop at The Armatura Press

The Armatura Press, 39–41 High Street,
Pewsey, Wiltshire UK

thearmaturapress.co.uk

THE ARMATVRA PRESS

Contents

Preface

Ut milites dicuntur, roughly 'as the soldiers are told/called', is a phrase from a 17th-century theologian, Johannes Piscator, but it can just as well be applied to what is nowadays referred to as the *sermo castrensis*, the camp argot, to distinguish it from the other variants of spoken (and written) Latin. The Roman army partly defined themselves by their language – Latin was used, even in areas where Greek was dominant – and mastering it was a requirement for any new recruit. This means that any reader confronting the Roman army for the first time – whether in fact, fiction, or on a visit to Hadrian's Wall – inevitably encounters a wealth of what appears to be technical terminology. What did it all mean? Even those with some knowledge may find themselves wondering what the source is for a particular term or phrase. This little book may well prove to be of some assistance, when much larger (and more expensive) tomes maintain an inscrutable silence; compiling it has certainly proved instructive to me.

Most of the terms in this dictionary were indeed used by the Romans, but some have been coined by scholars (in Latin) just to fill in the gaps and confuse things a little (*'lorica segmentata'* probably being the most famous, but there are others here). It is always important to be aware of the fact that Latin in particular could have many meanings for one word and that the Romans were often annoyingly imprecise in their technical usage of language (much to the evident frustration of those same Latin-wielding scholars). Loan (it is much politer than saying stolen or appropriated) words were common and Greece was generous in its vocabulary donations to the Roman army, in much the same way as it was with its art in the 2nd century BC. Arrian (himself writing in Greek) commented (Arr., *Tech. Takt.* 33–44) on how the Roman auxiliary cavalry terminology for the *hippika gymnasia* was almost entirely taken from the Celtic language, so the Greeks were far from being the only donors.

The present volume is inevitably heavily influenced by two previous publications. First is Frank Graham's *Dictionary of Roman Military Terms* and second Sander van Dorst's web page containing his *Glossary* of Greek and Latin military terms. However, neither of these provided sources for their entries and it always struck me as rather crucial to do so. When I came to produce my *Handbook to Roman Legionary Fortresses* (Bishop 2013), I included a brief yet pertinent glossary in the back that attempted to remedy this, and it struck me at the time that there was a need to do this for the Roman army in general, on a much broader scale.

This, then, is an exercitologist's guide to the terminology of the Roman army. There is no guarantee that the Romans themselves jargonised to the same extent as modern armies, but the rich and complex system of abbreviations they use on inscriptions might be thought to suggest that they did in this aspect at least. However, abbreviations only work if they are understood and the purpose of many inscriptions is to communicate to as wide an audience as possible, so it might be argued that whilst formal texts sought to cram as much as possible into as little space as was available, epitaphs wished for the widest readership possible so had to be decipherable by their target audience.

Acknowledgements

Several key individuals have helped this little book into existence and I should like to thank Drs Duncan Campbell and Jon Coulston for acting as alpha readers on the crucial dictionary section, and Simon Turney for acting as beta reader on the whole desperate mess. Finally, Lorraine Marlow has been kind enough to tolerate piles of books on the floor as I sought confirmation of the reality of some or other obscure term. I thank them all and remind you, patient reader, that all mistakes, clangers, and howlers remain the sole responsibility, nay, property of me.

Introduction

Each entry in what follows is set out according to a regular structure, so far as is possible:

- the term as a headword, followed by its gender (if a Latin substantive) and plural form (if any). Where an Anglicised form exists (e.g. 'centurion') this is indicated, as are modern coinages, such as the already mentioned 'lorica segmentata';
- the definition itself, with any subsidiary and associated definitions;
- sources for the use of the term are then provided from as wide a range of origins as possible, including literary, sub-literary, and epigraphic documents. For these, I have tried to use the least abbreviated (or reconstructed) forms possible, where inscriptions and sub-literary documents are concerned;
- finally, one pertinent modern (i.e. secondary) source is provided for each entry to allow further reading on that topic. Whilst these do not necessarily include the term in question, they will at least serve to provide context for it and its use. Together, they form a very basic core bibliography of popular works on the Roman army.

At the end of the book, a list of common epigraphic abbreviations for terms used by the army can be found, along with links to useful online resources, the bibliography, and – since dictionaries by definition do not need a conventional index – a set of subject indexes seeks to group the dictionary terms together appropriately.

A note on pronunciation

We have clues to how the Romans pronounced words and the components of those words, although even they seem to have got confused at times.

C and G were always hard (C was sometimes used interchangeably with the Greek-derived K), whilst V could be used as a consonant (similar to English W) or as a vowel (like English U), hence Valerius would be said (more or less) Walerius. TH seems to have been hard for some, so we find instances of 'Thracum' being written 'Tracum' (e.g. diploma *CIL* XVI, 54) or even 'Trhacum' (*CIL* XIII, 6286); whilst this last may simply be an error of transposition on the part of the letter-cutter, there are enough instances to suggest it may genuinely have reflected the way the word was pronounced. In contrast, PH seems readily to have been equated with F in some cases, as in *cataphractus/-fractus*. although the centurion Gellius Philippus, who helped construct Hadrian's Wall, had his *cognomen* spelled P(h)ilippus at least once (*RIB* 3407).

5

Some plural endings cause problems for the modern reader. The masculine plural -from -us (e.g. *legionarii* from *legionarius*) should have an 'ee' sound (and both syllables would be pronounced in that case, so it would have sounded like 'legio-nar-ee-ee'!. The feminine plural *-ae* from *a* (e.g. *lanceae* from *lancea*), on the other hand, had an 'eye' sound. This is more complex, as the first 'e' was probably said with something approaching an 'ay' sound, so 'lanc-ay-eye'. Fourth declension nouns that have an '-*ūs* plural form, such as *exercitūs* ('armies'), probably (but by no means definitely) rhymed with the English 'loose'. Y can cause problems, but just think of it as the English U (a clue here lies in the modern Arabic pronunciation of Syria as '*As-Sūrīyah*', but the Romans can also be caught writing it phonetically, as in the diploma *CIL* XVI, 106!).

Much more on pronunciation can be found in the excellent *Vox Latina* (Allen 1965) where all who struggle with their '*-ae*' and '*-i*' should go (and that includes most of the broadcast media).

Finally, and touchingly, it is amusing to note that case endings could cause problems even for Roman soldiers (not all of whom will have been native Latin speakers, of course). The bold '*vexillus*' on a sculpted panel of a *vexillum* from Corbridge (*RIB* 1154) can be matched by the letter written by the *decurio* Docilis to his commander where he appears to confuse the gender for *gladius* (*gladia instituta*: *AE* 1998, 839a)!

Abbreviations

abbr.	abbreviation	Aul. Gell.	Aulus Gellius, *Noctes*
Acta Max.	*Acta Maximiliani*		*Atticae*
adj.	adjective	*BCTH*	*Bulletin Archéologique*
AE	*L'Année Épigraphique*		*du Comité des Travaux*
alt.	alternative form		*Historiques*
Amm.	Ammianus Marcellinus,	*Bell. Afr.*	*De Bello Africo*
	Res Gestae	*BGU*	*Berliner griechische*
Ang.	Anglicised form		*Urkunden*
App.	Appian, *Historia Romana*	*BMC*	*Catalogue of the Roman*
	(Ρωμαϊκά)		*Empire Coins of the*
Apul., *Met.*	Apuleius, *Metamorphoses*		*British Museum*. Vols 1 to
Arr., *Ek.*	Arrian, *Ektaxis kat*		6, London
	Alanōn (Εκταξις κατά	Caes., *BC*	Caesar, *de Bello Civilo*
	Αλανών)	Caes., *BG*	Caesar, *de Bello Gallico*
Arr., *Tech. Takt.*	Arrian, *Technē Taktikē*	Caes., BH	Caesar, *de Bello*
	(Τέχνη Τακτική)		*Hispaniensi*

Cass. Dio	Cassius Dio, *Historia*
ChLA	*Chartae Latinae Antiquiores*
Cic., *Ad Fam.*	Cicero, *Ad Familiares*
Cic. *Catil.*	Cicero, *In Catilinam*
Cic., *Tusc.*	Cicero, *Tusculanae Disputationes*
Cic., Div.	Cicero, *De Divinatione*
Cic., Flac.	Cicero, *Pro Flacco*
Cic., Mil.	Cicero, *Pro Milone*
Cic., *Off.*	Cicero, *De Officiis*
Cic., *Phil.*	Cicero, *Philippicae*
Cic., *Pis.*	Cicero, *In Pisonem*
Cic., *Planc.*	Cicero, *Pro Plancio*
Cic., *Sull.*	Cicero, *Pro Sulla*
Cic., *Ver.*	Cicero, *In Verrem*
CIL	*Corpus Inscriptionum Latinarum*
Cod. Just.	*Codex Iustinianus*
Cod. Th.	*Codex Theodosianus*
Curt.	Curtius Rufus, *Historiarum Alexandri Magni*
DMC	*De Munificatio Castrensis*
Dig.	*Digesta*
Diocl.	Diocletian, *Edictum de Pretiis Venalium Rerum*
DRB	*De Rebus Bellicis*
f.	feminine noun
Fest.	Festus., *De Verborum Significatu*
FIRA	S. Riccobono and V. Arangio Ruiz (eds), *Fontes iuris romani anteiustiniani*
Front., *Strat.*	Frontinus, *Stratagemata*
Gaius	Gaius, *Institutionum*
Gk.	Greek
HA, *Aur.*	*Historia Augusta, Divus Aurelianus*
HA, *Hadr.*	*Historia Augusta, Hadrianus*
HA, *Macr.*	*Historia Augusta, Macrinus*
HA, *Pert.*	*Historia Augusta, Pertinax*
HA, *Pesc. Nig.*	*Historia Augusta, Pescennius Niger*
HA, *Sev. Alex.*	*Historia Augusta, Severus Alexander*
HA, Tac.	*Historia Augusta, Tacitus*
Hier., *CIH*	Hieronymus, *Contra Ioannem Hierosolymitanum Episcopum ad Pammachium*
Hor., Car.	Horace, Carmina
Isid., Orig.	Isidore, Origines
Justin, EHP	Iustini Historiarum Philippicarum: ex Trogo Pompeio (1829), Leipzig
Juv., Sat.	Juvenal, Saturae
Livy	Livy, Ab Urbe Condita Libri
Luc.	Lucan, de Bello Civili
m.	masculine noun
Mal., Chron.	John Malalas, Chronographia (Χρονογραφία)
Maur., Strat.	Maurice, Strategikon (Στρατηγικόν)
Mod.	modern coinage
n.	neuter noun
Nazar.	Nazarius, in Mynors 1964
ND	Notitia Dignitatum
Nep., Alc.	Cornelius Nepos, Alcibiades
O. Berenike	Bagnall *et al.* 2000
O. Bu Njem	Marichal 1992
O. Did.	Cuvigny 2012
Ov., Amor.	Ovid, Amores
Ov., Fast.	Ovid, Fasti
Pap. Bod.	Salomons 1996

7

part.	participle	Suet., *Cal.*	Suetonius, *Vita Gai*
Phr.	Phrase	Suet., *Claud.*	Suetonius, *Vita Divi*
pl.	plural form		*Claudi*
Plaut., *Curc.*	Plautus, *Curculio*	Suet., *Dom.*	Suetonius, *Vita Domitiani*
Plaut., *Ep.*	Plautus, *Epidicus*	Suet., *Galb.*	Suetonius, *Vita Galbae*
Plaut., *Poen.*	Plautus, *Poenulus*	Suet., *Iul.*	Suetonius, *Divi Iuli*
Pliny, *NH*	Pliny the Elder, *Naturalis*	Suet., *Otho*	Suetonius, *Othonis*
	Historiae	Suet., *Tib.*	Suetonius, *Tiberi*
Plut., *Marcell.*	Plutarch, *Bíoi parálleloi:*	Suet., *Vesp.*	Suetonius, *Vita Divi*
	Markellos (*Βίοι*		*Vespasiani*
	Παράλληλοι: Μάρκελλος)	Tab. Vind.	*Tabulae Vindolandenses*
Plut., *Marius*	Plutarch, *Bíoi parálleloi:*	Tac., *Ag.*	Tacitus, *Agricola*
	Marios (*Βίοι*	Tac., *Ann.*	Tacitus, *Annales*
	Παράλληλοι: Μάριος)	Tac., *Ger.*	Tacitus, *Germanica*
P. Col.	Columbia papyrus	Tac., *Hist.*	Tacitus, *Historiae*
	(Gillam 1967)	Ulp.	Ulpian, *Liber Singularis*
P. Mich. 8	*Michigan Papyri 8*		*Regularum*
	(Youtie and Winter 1951)	Val. Max.	Valerius Maximus,
Pap. Choix	*Choix de Papyrus Grecs*		*Factorum et Dictorum*
	(Bingen *et al.* 1968)		*Memorabilium*
Polyb.	Polybios, *Historiai*	Varro, *LL*	Varro, *Lingua Latina*
Prud., *Psych.*	Prudentius,	Varro, *RR*	Varro, *Rerum Rusticarum*
	Psychomachia	Veg., *DRM*	Vegetius, *De Re Militaris*
RIB	*Roman Inscriptions of*	Veg., *Mul.*	Vegetius, *Mulomedicina*
	Britain (I, 1965; II,	Vell. Pat.	Velleius Paterculus,
	1990–5; III, 2009), Oxford		*Historiae*
RIC	*Roman Imperial Coinage*	Verg., *Aen.*	Vergil, *Aeneis*
RMR	*Roman Military Records*	Verg., *Georg.*	Vergil, *Georgica*
	(Fink 1971)	Vitr.	Vitruvius, *De*
Sall., *Hist.*	Sallust, *Historiarum*		*Architectura*
	Fragmenta	Vulg., *1 Sam.*	Vulgate Bible, *Liber*
Sall., *Iug.*	Sallust, *Bellum*		*Samuhelis* (1 Samuel)
	Iugurthinum	Xen., *Anab.*	Xenophon, *Anabasis*
Sen., *De Ben.*	Seneca, *De Beneficiis*	Xen. *Peri Hipp.*	Xenophon, *Peri Hippikes*
Sen., *Epist.*	Seneca, *Epistulae*	ZPE	*Zeitschrift für*
	Morales ad Lucilium		*Papyrologie und*
Sil. Ital., *Pun.*	Silius Italicus, *Punica*		*Epigraphik*
Suet., *Aug.*	Suetonius, *Vita Divi*		
	Augusti		

Dictionary

accensus (m. pl. *accensi*) A member of the *accensi*, who were light-armed troops stationed behind the *triarii* in the Republican *acies* and usually equipped in a similar manner to the *rorarii*. Possibly supernumeraries, such as camp-followers and slaves. Livy 1.43.8. [Keppie 1984]

acies (f. pl. *acies*) Literally 'a blade's edge'. A battle line (Veg., *DRM* 3.14; Cic., *Fam.* 10.30.2); **simplex a.**: a single battle line (one row of ten cohorts) (*Bell. Afr.* 13; 59; Caes., *BG* 3.22.1); **duplex a.** a double battle line (e.g. ten cohorts arrayed in two lines of five) (Caes., *BC* 3.67.4); **triplex a.** a triple battle line (four cohorts in the front line, three in the second, and three in the third) (Caes., *BC* 1.83.2). [Cowan 2007]

acta (f. pl. n/a) An account of the finances, posts, and numbers of each legion. Veg., *DRM* 2.19; *RMR* 99.1.7. See also **pridianum**. [Fink 1971]

act(u)arius (m. pl. *act(u)arii*) A Late Roman clerk in the *officium legionis*, principally involved with compilation of the *acta*. *CIL* XIII, 7750; *RIB* 1101. [Fink 1971]

adiutor (m. pl. *adiutores*). Literally 'helper' or 'assistant'. A clerk. *AE* 1898, 19; 1909,3. [Goldsworthy 2003]

adlocutio (alt. *allocutio* f. pl. *adlocutiones*) An address or harangue, usually by an emperor, to troops (e.g. Hadrian at Lambaesis), often depicted on coins and in public sculpture. *CIL* VIII, 2532. [Goldsworthy 2003]

ad nomen respondere (Phr.): A muster or roll-call of troops, associated with pay parades (Veg., *DRM* 3.4 has an alternative version: *ad nomen observare*). Livy 28.29.12. [Goldsworthy 2003]

ad signa convenire (Phr.): Re-assemble. Caes., *BG* 6.37. See also **signa convertere** [Goldsworthy 2003]

An **adlocutio** *depicted on Trajan's Column.*

ad triarios redire (Phr.): Literally 'To reach the *triarii*' with the sense of a serious situation, since the *triarii* were not normally needed in battle. Livy 8.8.11. [Keppie 1984]

adventus (m. pl. *adventūs*): Ceremonial arrival of a military expedition, under the Republic of consuls, under the Empire of the emperor. Livy 22.61.13; *RIC* 554. [Goldsworthy 2003]

aedes (principiorum) (pl.) Shrine of the standards, in the centre of the rear range of rooms in the *principia* (*RIB* 3027). See also *sacellum* [Johnson 1983]

aedituus (m. pl. *aeditui*): Keeper of a shrine or temple. RMR 47; *CIL* III, 5822. [Goldsworthy 2003]

aerarium militare (n. pl. n/a) The military treasury. It was set up by Augustus with his own money to fund soldiers' discharge grants. Administered by three prefects, it was supported by a 5% inheritance tax. Suet., *Aug.* 49; Cass. Dio 55.25; Tac., *Ann.* 1.78. [Keppie 1984]

aerarius (m. pl. *aerarii*): Bronze smith (*Dig.* 50.6.7; *AE* 1995, 1351). [Goldsworthy 2003]

aerorum see *aerum*

aerum (Phr.): Literally 'of annual payments', used with a number of years on tombstones to indicate length of military service. *RIB* 201; *CIL* XIII, 12086. See also *militavit* and *stipendiorum* [Goldsworthy 2003]

aestivalium (f. pl. *aestivalia*) A summer or campaign camp with tented accommodation. In the Principate, multiple legions might share such a base. *DMC* 45; 48. See also *castra aestiva* and **temporary camp**. [Jones 2012]

agentes in praesidio (pl. Phr.): Troops acting in place of the regular garrison.

RIB 1583. [Goldsworthy 2003]

agentes in rebus (pl. Phr.). Part of the internal imperial security service, organised on military lines. Fourth-century replacements for the *frumentarii*. Amm. 14.11.23; *ND Or.* 11.11. [Goldsworthy 2003]

agger (m. pl. *aggeri*): 1. A siege ramp (Caes., *BG* 2.12.5; 7.24; Veg., *DRM* 4.15); 2. a synonym for a *tribunal* (Tac. *Ann.* 1.18); 3. a rampart around a camp (Caes., *BG* 7.72). [Campbell 2003]

agmen (n. pl. *agmines*): A column of troops, usually on the march (Sall., *Iug.* 46.6); *a. iustum*: a column in close order (Tac., *Hist.* 1.68); *a. extremum*: rearguard (Tac., *Hist.* 4.22); *a. primum*: vanguard (Livy 34.28.5); *a. quadratum*: column in square formation (Sall., *Iug.* 100.1). [Cowan 2007]

agrimensor see *mensor*

ala (f. pl. *alae*): Literally 'a wing'; 1. in the Republican period, a flanking cavalry force in the battle line, usually composed of *socii* (Caes., *BG* 1.51; Cic., *Off.* 2.45); 2. more generally, the flanks (or wings) of a battle line or battlefield formation (Aul. Gell. 10.9.1; Livy 31.21.7); 3. in the Principate (and later), an auxiliary cavalry unit, either normal- (*quingenaria*) or double-strength (*milliaria*), the former being commanded by a *praefectus alae* or *equitum* and the latter a *tribunus alae* or *equitum* (*DMC* 16; Tac., *Hist.* 1.59; *RIB* 159; *CIL* XVI, 69). [Cowan 2007]

albata decursio (Phr.): Participating in a *decursio* wearing white clothing, only rarely granted and usually by an emperor. *CIL* III, 14387; *AE* 2006, 1480. [Goldsworthy 2003]

ambulatum (n. pl. *ambulata*) A regular

route march undertaken by units as part of their training. Veg., *DRM* 1.27. See also *ambulatura* [Goldsworthy 2003]

ambulatura (f. pl. *ambulaturae* Mod.) A regular route march undertaken by units as part of their training. See also *ambulatum* [Goldsworthy 2003]

amentum (n. pl. *amenta*): A throwing strap which, when wrapped around a javelin, imparted both spin and greater range. Festus s.v. *Amenta*; Caes., *BG* 5.48.5; Verg., *Aen.* 9.665. [Bishop and Coulston 2006]

amphitheatrum (n. pl. *amphitheatra*) An amphitheatre, often found in association with fortresses and some forts, as well as in civilian contexts. Possibly used for training and other military purposes, as well as for gladiatorial contests and wild beast hunts. *AE* 1955, 135. See also *ludus* [Johnson 1983]

annona (f. pl. *annonae*): Rations (Caes., *BC* 1.52; Veg., *DRM* 1.19); *a. militaris*: Rations issued to the army without deductions from pay, introduced in the 3rd century AD and funded by taxes in kind (*HA, Sev. Alex.* 15.5). [Goldsworthy 2003]

antesignanus (m. pl. *antesignani*): Literally 'before the standards', troops stationed in front of the standards, used sometimes synonymously with 'skirmisher'. Caes., *BC* 1.43.3; Livy 22.5.7; *AE* 1978, 471. [Goldsworthy 2003]

aquaeductus (m. pl. *aquaeductūs*): A channel bringing water into a fortification. *CIL* XIII, 11759; *RIB* 430. [Johnson 1983]

aquila (f. pl. *aquilae*) The legionary eagle standard, made of silver or gold, and carried by the *aquilifer*, who was a member of the first cohort of the legion. Tac., *Ann.* 1.39; Cass. Dio 40.18; *AE* 1993, 1571. See also *natalis aquilae* [Bishop and Coulston 2006]

aquilifer (m. pl. *aquiliferi*) Standard-bearer charged with the care of the *aquila*. Veg., *DRM* 2.7; 2.13; *CIL* XIII, 6901; Caes., *BG* 5.37.5. [Goldsworthy 2003]

arcanus (m. pl. *arcani*): An organisation of scouts in Roman Britain, disbanded by Theodosius after they became corrupt. Ammianus refers to them as '*areani*' which has been assumed to be a scribal error, but there appears to be sub-literary corroboration for the name. Amm. 28.3.8; *Tab. Vind.* 162. [Goldsworthy 2003]

architectus (m. pl. *architecti*) An engineer. The term had a wide range of applications, from lime-burning, to artillery, to tunnelling expertise (*RIB* 1542; *Dig.* 50.6.7); *a. armamentarius Imperatoris*: engineer in the armoury in Rome (*CIL* VI, 2725; tombstone depicting a catapult). [Goldsworthy 2003]

arcuarius (m. pl. *arcuarii*) A bow-maker. *Dig.* 50.6.7. [Goldsworthy 2003]

arcus (m. pl. *arcus*) A bow. The Roman army made widespread use of the Eastern composite bow. Veg., *DRM* 1.15; 20. [Bishop and Coulston 2006]

areani see *arcanus*

aries (m. pl. *arietes*): Literally 'a ram', this was a battering ram, used in attacking besieged fortifications by breaching walls or breaking through gates. Veg., *DRM* 4.14; Vitr. 10.13. [Campbell 2003]

arma (n. pl.) Literally 'weapons'. 1. The area in front of a tent set aside for the storage of weapons. *DMC* 1. 2. By association with 1., the front room of a barrack room-pair. [Johnson 1983]

armamentarium (n. pl. *armamentaria*): A structure that served as an armoury. *RIB* 1092; *AE* 1984, 703. [Johnson 1983]

armatura (f. pl. *armaturae*): Weapons training, which included practice with double-weight sword and shield at the *palus*. Veg., *DRM* 1.13; 2.23; Amm. 14.11. [Goldsworthy 2003]

armicustos (m. pl. *armicustodes*): An *immunis* with a *classis* equivalent to the *custos armorum* in land units. *CIL* XI, 67; *AE* 1905, 201. See also *custos armorum* [Goldsworthy 2003]

armilla (f. pl. *armillae*): Bracelet of bronze, silver, or gold awarded for bravery. Livy 10.44.3; *AE* 1913, 48. [Maxfield 1981]

armillata (adj.): Title awarded to a unit that received a block grant of the *armilla*, first attested in the Trajanic period. *AE* 1930, 92; 1939, 81a. [Maxfield 1981]

armilustrium (n. pl. *armilustria*): Festival held on the 19th October, possibly marking the end of the campaigning season. Varro, *LL* 5.3. [Goldsworthy 2003]

armorum custos see *custos armorum*

ascensus (m. pl. *ascensūs*): Stairway or ramp giving access to the top of a fortification. *DMC* 58. [Johnson 1983]

asinarius (m. pl. *asinarii*): A muleteer. *RMR* 9.12 [Goldsworthy 2003]

auxilia (n. pl.): Auxiliary troops, complementary to the legions, providing light infantry, cavalry, and specialist missile troops such as archers (Caes., *BG* 3.23; Veg., *DRM* 2.2); *a. palatina*: Late Roman infantry units, part of the field army with, but distinct from, the *comitatenses* (*ND Or.* 5; *Occ.* 5). [Goldsworthy 2003]

auxiliarius (m. pl. *auxiliarii*): A member

of the *auxilia*. Livy 44.4.11; Tac., *Ann.* 1.56; *Hist.* 2.68. [Goldsworthy 2003]

ballista (f. pl. *ballistae*): Before Trajan, a torsion-powered, twin-armed, stone-throwing catapult, but later used for a bolt-shooter. Vitr. 10.11; Veg., *DRM* 4.22. [Bishop and Coulston 2006]

ballistarium (n. pl. *ballistaria*): Perhaps an emplacement for a *ballista*, but more likely where they were stored. Plaut., *Poen.* 1.1.74; *RIB* 1280–1. [Johnson 1983]

ballistarius (m. pl. *ballistarii*): Member of a *ballista* crew. Veg., *DRM* 2.2; Amm. 16.2.5. [Goldsworthy 2003]

balneum (n. pl. *balnea*). The fort or fortress baths. *CIL* III, 10489; *RMR* 47.9. [Johnson 1983]

balteus (m. pl. *baltei*) A waist belt, often decorated with metal plates, sometimes used to attach the sword and dagger scabbards. Caes., *BG* 5.44.7; Pliny, *NH* 33.58; Tac., *Hist.* 1.57. See also *cingulum militare* [Bishop and Coulston 2006]

barritus (m. pl. *barritus*): War cry derived from that of German warriors. Veg., *DRM* 3.18; Amm. 16.12.43. [Goldsworthy 2003]

basilica (f. pl. *basilicae*): 1. A hall, with a nave and two aisles, found associated in a military context with *balnea* and *principia* (*RIB* 605; 1091; 3027); 2. a building wherein soldiers could train under cover in bad weather (Veg., *DRM* 2.23); *b. equestris exercitatoria*: a building wherein cavalry could train under cover in bad weather, and possibly to be equated with the **forehall** in a fort (*RIB* 978). [Johnson 1983]

Batavus (pl.): Nickname for a member of both the *Germani corporis custodes* and the later *equites singularis Augusti*. Cass. Dio 55.24.6; Suet., *Cal.* 43. [Speidel 1984]

beneficiarius (m. pl. *beneficiarii*): A detached legionary soldier performing a special task, usually assigned to a senior officer (Fest. s.v.; Veg., *DRM* 2.7; Caes., *BC* 1.75); *b. consularis*: attached to a *legatus Augusti pro praetore* (*CIL* III, 3397; *AE* 1994, 1424); *b. legati legionis*: attached to a *legatus legionis* (*CIL* XIII, 1797; *AE* 1984, 739); *b. legionis*: attached to a legion (*CIL* XII, 164; *AE* 1968, 605); *b. officii praesidis* attached to the *officium* of a *praeses* (*CIL* V, 8275); *b. praefecti*: attached to a *praefectus* (*CIL* III, 13419; VI, 3511); *b. praefecti praetorio*: attached to a *praefectus praetorio* (*CIL* XI, 395; IX, 5839); *b. praesidis*: attached to a *praeses* (*CIL* III, 252; VIII, 9380); *b. procuratoris* attached to a *procurator* (*AE* 1904, 177; *CIL* XIII, 1856); *b. subpraefecti*: attached to a *subpraefectus* (CIL VI, 37295); *b. tribuni*: attached to a *tribunus* (*CIL* III, 7334; *AE* 1933, 87). [Goldsworthy 2003]

biarchus (n. pl. *biarchi*): Under the Late Empire, possibly in charge of a *contubernium* and thus equivalent to the *caput contubernii* or the *decanus*. On double pay, so similar to a *duplicarius*. Hier., *CIH* 19; *AE* 1891, 105; *CIL* V, 08755. [Goldsworthy 2003]

biremis (f. pl. *biremes* Ang. 'bireme'): A warship with two levels of rowers. Tac., *Hist.* 5.23. See also *liburna* [Goldsworthy 2003]

bis armillata (adj.): Unit twice awarded the *armilla*. *AE* 1930, 92. [Maxfield 1981]

bona castrensia (f. pl. *bonae castrensiae*): A soldier's possessions accumulated during his service with the army. *Dig.*

42.6.1. See also *peculium castrense* [Brand 1968]

bis torquata (adj.): Unit twice awarded the *torques*. *AE* 1930, 92; 1980, 496; CIL XI, 5669. [Maxfield 1981]

bracae (f. pl.): Trousers or leggings. Tac., *Hist.* 2.20; *HA, Sev. Alex.* 40.5; *P. Mich.* 8.467.22. [Sumner 2009]

brevis (n. pl. *breves*): Unit summary roll under the Dominate. Veg., *DRM* 2.19; *HA, Sev. Alex.* 21. [Fink 1971]

buccellarius (m. pl. *buccellarii* Mod. deduced from 6th century term): Literally 'biscuit man', a member of a private army in the Late Empire. See also *foederatus* [Southern and Dixon 1996]

buc(c)ellatum (n. pl. *buccellata*): Biscuits issued to soldiers as rations. Amm. 17.8.2; *HA, Pesc. Nig.* 10.4. [Goldsworthy 2003]

bucculla (f. pl. *buccullae*): Helmet cheekpiece. Juv., *Sat.* 10.34. [Bishop and Coulston 2006]

buc(c)ina (f. pl. *buc(c)inae*): Horn. Used to sound the watches, hence third watch was *tertia bucina*. Livy 26.15. [Goldsworthy 2003]

buc(c)inator (m. pl. *buc(c)inatores*): Musician who played the *buc(c)ina*. *Dig.* 50.6.7; *AE* 1908, 272; 1976, 642. [Goldsworthy 2003]

burgus (m. pl. *burgi*): Small tower or fortification. Veg., *DRM* 4.10; *CIL* III, 88. [Johnson 1983]

caetra (f. pl. *caetrae*): Small shield, originally Spanish. Livy 21.27.5; Tac., *Ag.* 36. [Bishop and Coulston 2006]

caetratus (m. pl. *caetrati*): Literally, 'small-shielded', used synonymously with 'lightly armed' or 'light troops' (i.e. skirmishers). Livy 31.36.1; 33.4.4; Caes., *BC* 1.70.4. [Goldsworthy 2003] *calceus* (m. pl. *calcei*): Boot. Juv., *Sat.* 16.13. [Bishop and Coulston 2006]

calciarium (n. pl. *calciaria*): Allowance for shoes, requested by sailors from Vespasian. Suet., *Vesp.* 8. [Goldsworthy 2003]

caliga (f. pl. *caligae*): Military boot associated with ordinary soldiers. Juv., *Sat.* 16.25; Tac., *Ann.* 1.41; *CIL* IX, 5840. [Bishop and Coulston 2006]

caligatus (m. pl. *caligati*): An ordinary soldier. Suet., *Aug.* 25.3; *AE* 1990, 896; *CIL* VI, 37245a. See also *miles gregarius* and *eques gregarius* [Goldsworthy 2003]

calo (m. pl. *calones*): Slave acting as a soldier's servant. Liv. 9.37.8; Caes., *BG* 6.36.1; Tac., *Hist.* 3.33. See also *lixa* [Goldsworthy 2003]

campestres (pl.): Deities with a Celtic origin, associated with the army and the *campus* and sometimes equated with the three mother goddesses. *CIL* VI, 768; *RIB* 1334; 2121. [Goldsworthy 2003]

campicursio (f. pl. *campicursiones*): Mentioned by Vegetius and described as 'an inspection of arms'. Veg., *DRM* 3.4. See also *decursio* [Goldsworthy 2003]

campidoctor (m. pl. *campidoctores*): Literally 'exercise ground instructor'. Drill instructor. Veg., *DRM* 3.6; Amm. 15.3.10; *CIL* II, 4083. [Goldsworthy 2003]

campus (m. pl. *campi*) Usually translated as 'parade ground' but probably more accurately 'exercise ground' or 'training area'. *CIL* VIII, 2532. [Johnson 1983]

canabae (f. pl.): Literally 'booths'. A term often applied to the civil settlement outside a legionary base. *CIL* III, 6166; 7474. [Johnson 1983]

Cantabricus (m. pl. *Cantabrici*):

Otherwise known as the Cantabrian circle, part of the *hippika gymnasia*, whereby cavalry circled whilst throwing javelins at their opponents (Arr., *Tech. Tak.* 43; *CIL* VIII, 2532) [Hyland 1993]

capitulum (n. pl. *capitula*): The frame of a *ballista*. Vitr. 1.1; 10.12; *ChLA* 10.409.2.15. [Bishop and Coulston 2006]

capsarius (m. pl. *capsarii*): Medic. *Dig.* 50.6.7; *CIL* XIII, 5623. [Goldsworthy 2003]

capulus (m. pl. *capuli*): A sword hilt. Pliny, *NH* 33.58; Tac., *Ann.* 2.21; Fest. s.v. [Bishop and Coulston 2006]

caput porci(num) (n. pl. *capita porcorum*): Literally 'pig's head', an informal term referring to the battlefield tactic known as the *cuneus*. Veg., *DRM* 3.19; Amm. 17.13.9. [Cowan 2007]

carcer (m. pl. *carceres*): Prison. *O. Bu Njem* 8; *AE* 1990, 896. [Johnson 1983]

carcerarius (m. pl. *carcerarii*): Prison-keeper. *CIL* III, 10493k; *AE* 1978, 730. [Goldsworthy 2003]

carpentarius (m. pl. *carpentarii*): Wagon-maker or -driver. *Dig.* 50.6.7. [Goldsworthy 2003]

carrarius (m. pl. *carrarii*): Wagon-maker or -driver. *Tab. Vind.* 185; 309. [Goldsworthy 2003]

carroballista (f. pl. *carroballistae*): Bolt-shooting *ballista* mounted on a cart. Veg., *DRM* 2.25; 3.24. [Bishop and Coulston 2006]

cassis (f. pl. *cassides*): Helmet (of metal, according to the late Isid., *Orig.* 18.14.1). Juv., *Sat.* 10.34; Caes., *BG* 7.45. See also *galea* [Bishop and Coulston 2006]

castellum (n. pl. *castella*): Diminutive form of *castra*, used of what are nowadays termed 'forts'. Veg., *DRM* 3.8; Tac., *Ag.* 1.20; *AE* 2001, 1978. [Johnson 1983]

A **carroballista** *depicted on Trajan's Column*

castigatio (f. pl. *castigationes*):
Chastisement or verbal rebuke for
soldiers. *Dig.* 49.16.3; Vell. Pat. 2.114.3.
[Goldsworthy 2003]

castra (n. pl.): Camp or fortification
under the later Republic and Principate;
c. aestiva: Literally 'summer camp', a
campaign camp (Tac., *Ann.* 1.16; 1.37);
c. hiberna: winter quarters, used of what
are nowadays called 'fortresses' and
'forts' (*AE* 1948, 120; 1964, 148); *c.
peregrinorum*: Base on the Caelian Hill
for provincial troops visiting Rome
(Amm. 16.12.66; *CIL* VI, 231; 36775);
c. praetoria: Base for the *praetoriae
cohortes* situated on the north-western
outskirts of Rome and constructed with
defences of brick-faced concrete under
Tiberius (Tac., *Ann.* 4.1–2; Pliny, *NH*
3.30 *CIL* VI, 2843); *c. stativa*: Catch-all
term for temporary and permanent
fortifications such as *c. aestiva* and
hiberna (Veg., *DRM* 3.8; Tac., *Ann.*
3.21). [Johnson 1983]

castrense peculium see *peculium
castrense*

castris (adj.): Literally 'from camp'. Used
of a soldier born in a military settlement
(*RMR* 39.4; *CIL* VIII, 2567).
[Goldsworthy 2003]

castrum (also *kastrum* n. pl. *castra*): Early
Republican and Late Roman term for a
fortification. Nep., *Alc.* 9.3; *AE* 2003,
1532; *RIB* 721; *CIL* VIII, 4354. [Johnson
1983]

catafracta (f. pl. *catafractae*): Armour. Tac.,
Hist. 1.79; Veg., *DRM* 1.20; 2.14. See also
lorica [Bishop and Coulston 2006]

catafractarius see cataphractarius

catafractus see *cataphractus*

cataphractarius (m. pl. *cataphractarii*):
Armoured cavalryman. *HA, Alex. Sev.* 56;
Amm. 16.2.5; *CIL* V, 6784. See also
cataphractus [Goldsworthy 2003]

cataphractus (m. pl. *cataphracti*):
Armoured cavalryman. Livy 35.48.3;
CIL V, 6784. See also *cataphractarius*
[Goldsworthy 2003]

catapulta (f. pl. *catapultae*): Torsion
artillery weapon, possibly covering both
stone-throwing and bolt-shooting ma-
chines. Vitr., 10.11–13; Caes., *BC* 2.9.4.

Pinnae *of the* **Castra Praetoria** *embedded within the Aurelian Walls of Rome*

[Bishop and Coulston 2006]
causaria missio (f. pl. *causariae missiones*): Invaliding out before completion of a soldier's term of service. This apparently still counted as a form of *honesta missio. Dig.* 49.16.13; *CIL* VI, 3373; *AE* 2007, 1224. See also *causarius*, *honesta missio* and *ignominiosa missio* [Brand 1968]

causarius (m. pl. *causarii*): A soldier invalided out as *causaria missio*. Livy 6.6.14; *Dig.* 3.2.2; *AE* 2007, 1224; 2006, 1833. See also *causaria missio* [Brand 1968]

cedo alteram see *vitis*

centenarius (m. pl. *centenarii*): Late Roman equivalent to *centurio*. Also a procuratorial salary grade. Veg., *DRM* 2.13; *CIL* V, 8758. [Goldsworthy 2003]

cento (m. pl. *centones*): 1. a form of head covering (possibly a bandana) worn under the helmet (Amm. 19.8.8); 2. a rag, which as part of a patchwork, was used to cover the *vinea* (Veg., *DRM* 4.15). [Goldsworthy 2003]

centuria (f. pl. *centuriae*): 1. A sub-unit of a

cohors, originally 100 (and fossilised in Veg., *DRM* 2.8), but by the time of the Principate, only 80 *milites*. (*DMC* 1). It comprised ten *contubernia*, a *centurio*, an *optio*, and a *signifer*. 2. By extension, a barrack block intended to house 1 (*RIB* 334). [Keppie 1984]

centurio (m. pl. *centuriones* Ang. centurion): The commander of a *centuria*. In the Principate, distinguished by a *crista transversa*, a *vitis*, and wearing the sword on the opposite side to his men (Veg., *DRM* 2.8; 2.13; *RIB* 203; *CIL* III, 4060.); *c. exercitator*: in charge of trainers (*CIL* VI, 224); *c. exercitator equitum*: in charge of horse (or cavalry) training (*CIL* XI, 395); *c. princeps*: see *princeps*; *c. supernumerarius*: a centurion not in post, e.g. in charge of training legionary cavalry as a *magister equitum* (*CIL* V, 8278). [Keppie 1984]

cerarius (m. pl. *cerarii*): A clerk who wrote upon wax tablets. *CIL* VIII, 2986. [Goldsworthy 2003]

cervus (m. pl. *cervi*): Literally 'stag', a palisade, obstacle, or *chevaux-de-frise*

pilus posterior	princeps posterior	hastatus posterior
pilus prior	princeps prior	hastatus prior

Diagram illustrating the hierarchy of centurions in cohorts II to X.

formed from sharpened stakes. Caes., *BG* 7.72; Livy 44.11.4. [Goldsworthy 2003]

cibaria (n. pl.): Rations, a deduction for which was made from each instalment of pay. Suet., *Gal.* 7.2; Liv. 21.49.8; *O. Did.* 455.4–5. [Goldsworthy 2003]

cingulum militiae (n. pl. *cingula militiae*): Late Roman term for the military belt. *Cod. Just.* 7.38.1; 12.23.9; 12.37.16.7. [Bishop and Coulston 2006]

cippus (m. pl. *cippi*): Literally 'grave-marker' or 'boundary post', an obstacle formed from a sharpened tree trunk or branch, sunk into a trench. Several rows of trenches could overlap to form an entanglement. Caes., *BG* 7.73. [Goldsworthy 2003]

circitor (m. *circitores*): A post in a Late Roman cavalry unit, responsible for the rounds of sentries, similar to the *tesserarius*. Hier., *CIH* 19; Veg., *DRM* 3.8; *AE* 1912, 192; *CIL* V, 6784; XIII, 3457. [Southern and Dixon 1996]

circumvallatus (adj.): Surrounded by a circumvallation; a fortification constructed by a besieging army around the object of their siege. Caes., *BG* 7.44.3; Livy 43.19.9. [Campbell 2003]

civium Romanorum (pl.): A block grant of Roman citizenship to an auxiliary unit given as an award. Not granted after the *constitutio Antoniniana*. *CIL* II, 4114; XVI, 69. See also *constitutio Antoniniana* [Goldsworthy 2003]

classiarius (m. pl. *classiarii*): A marine (a soldier serving in a fleet). Caes., *BC* 3.100; Suet., *Tib.* 62.2; *AE* 1990, 870. [Goldsworthy 2003]

classicum (n. pl. *classica*): A military fanfare, sounded when an *imperator* was present or when capital punishment was to be enacted. It was sounded on the *cornu*, according to Vegetius (although he wrote by *bucinatores*). Veg., *DRM* 2.22. [Goldsworthy 2003]

classis (f. pl. *classes*): 1. The early Roman army (Aul. Gell. 10.15; Festus s. v. *procincta classis*); 2. one of the five classes within the early Roman army (Livy 1.42.5; Cic., *Phil.* 2.33); 3. a fleet. Under the Principate, the term covered the two praetorian fleets – the *c. Misenensis* (*CIL* III, 1919) and *c. Ravennatis* (*CIL* XIII, 1770) – and the various provincial maritime and riverine fleets: *c. Britannica* (*AE* 1987, 796), *c. Germanica* (*CIL* XII, 681), *c. Moesica* (*CIL* IX, 3609), *c. Pontica* (*CIL* VI, 41271), *c. Syriaca* (*CIL* III, 434). [Goldsworthy 2003]

clavarium (n. pl. *clavaria*): A donative given towards the cost of nails for hob-nailed boots. Tac., *Hist.* 3.50. [Goldsworthy 2003]

clavicula (f. pl. *claviculae*): Literally 'little key'. A type of temporary camp gateway consisting of an earthwork bank in the form of a quarter circle. Excavated examples are frequently accompanied by a ditch. *DMC* 55. [Jones 2012]

clavicularius (m. pl. *clavicularii*): A jailer. *CIL* III, 3484. [Goldsworthy 2003]

clepsydra (f. pl. *clepsydrae* Gk. κλεψύδρα): A water clock. Veg., *DRM* 3.8. See also *horologium* [Johnson 1983]

clibanarius (m. pl. *clibanarii*): Literally 'oven-man'. Heavy cavalry, completely enclosed in armour. The term is derived from a portable oven or *clibanus*. Amm. 16.10.8; Nazar. 22.4; *HA*, *Alex. Sev.* 56.5. [Goldsworthy 2003]

clipeus (m. pl. *clipei*): A circular shield, resembling the Greek *aspis*. By the 1st century AD, generally only referring to votive shields, such as the *c. virtutis*. Livy 1.43.2; Verg., *Aen.* 2.443; *AE* 1952, 165. [Bishop and Coulston 2006]

cohors (f. pl. *cohortes* Ang. cohort) 1. A sub-unit of a *legio*, normally comprising six *centuriae* (although the First Cohort comprised five double strength *centuriae*) (Veg., *DRM* 2.6; *DMC* 2–3); 2. an auxiliary infantry or part-mounted unit, either normal- or double-strength (*AE* 1994, 1303); *c. equitata*: a part-mounted unit with both infantry and cavalry (*DMC* 19; *CIL* XI, 7427; *AE* 1925, 44); *c. legionaria*: a legionary cohort, as distinct from any other sort (*DMC* 4); *c. milliaria*: A cohort of ten *centuriae*, or 800 men (*DMC* 28; *AE* 2003, 1440); *c. peditata*: An infantry unit (*DMC* 19; *CIL* III, 3318; XVI, 112); *c. praetoria*: A sub-unit of the Praetorian Guard, formed under Augustus; there were originally nine and later up to sixteen (under Vitellius) *cohortes praetoriae* (*DMC* 6; Tac., *Ann.* 4.5.3; *CIL* VI, 2442); *c. quingenaria*: a normal-strength unit of six *centuriae*, or 480 men (*DMC* 28; *AE* 1983, 851b); *c. sagittariorum* a unit of archers (*CIL* III, 600; *RIB* 1778); *c. voluntariorum* A unit of Roman citizens serving as *auxilia* (*AE* 1994, 1303; *CIL* III, 386a). [Keppie 1984]

cohortalis (m. pl. *cohortales*): A soldier serving in a *cohors* of the *auxilia*. Often used as a substantive derived from ***miles***

A grafitto from Dura-Europos thought to depict a **clibanarius***.*

c. or ***eques c***. ChLA 10.409.2.5. [Goldsworthy 2003]

collegium (n. pl. *collegia*): An association of military personnel (such as *cornicines* or *optiones*) in *scholae* as social gatherings. *Dig.* 47.22.1; *CIL* VIII, 2557; XIII, 7754 [Goldsworthy 2003]

colonia (f. pl. *coloniae* Ang. colony): A formal settlement for ***veterani***. Tac., *Ann.* 14.31; *RIB* 161. [Keppie 1984]

comes (m. pl. *comites* Ang. count): 1. A companion or advisor of a commander, notably of an emperor (Suet., *Caes.* 42); 2. A high-ranking official under the Late Empire, such as the *c. littoris Saxonici per Britanniam* (*ND Occ.* 28.1; cf. Amm. 27.8.1). [Southern and Dixon 1996]

comitatensis (m. pl. *comitatenses*): A member of the *comitatus*, who were mobile troops assigned to escort the emperor on campaign. *Cod. Th.* 7.1.18; 7.20.4.2; *CIL* IX, 5649. [Southern and Dixon 1996]

comitatus (m. pl. *comitatūs*): A mobile field army of the Late Roman period, established by the time of Constantine

ROMAN LEGIONARY COHORTS

ENEMY

Diagram illustrating cohort deployment

and possibly introduced by Diocletian, and divided between infantry, commanded by a *magister peditum*, and cavalry, under the command of a *magister equitum* (*Acta Max.* 2.9; *CIL* III, 6194; *AE* 1949, 38). [Southern and Dixon 1996]

commeatus (m. pl. *commeati*): Military leave or furlough. Tac., *Hist.* 1.46; Livy 1.57; *Tab. Vind.* 175. [Goldsworthy 2003]

commentariensis (m. pl. *commentarienses*): A clerk who maintained a list of soldiers. *CIL* VIII, 2812. [Fink 1971]

commilito (m. pl. *commilitones*): Literally 'fellow soldier', a term often used by emperors trying to endear themselves to troops through association. Suet., *Claud.* 10; Livy 3.50.5. See also *frater* [Goldsworthy 2003]

concessa consuetudo (Phr.): An informal union between a soldier and a woman equivalent to (but without the legal force of) marriage, so probably cohabitation. *AE* 1979, 626; 1985, 994. [Phang 2001]

Concordia (f. no pl.): Harmony, a minor goddess whose invocation is nowadays suspected to be indicative of a lack of same between units. HA, *Tac.* 2; *RIB* 1125; 3459; *RIC* 5.224. [Goldsworthy 2003]

coniunx (f. pl. *coniuges*): 1. A wife, so in a legal union with a veteran soldier (*RIB* 363; *CIL* VI, 3585); 2. a concubine or common-law wife, cohabiting with a soldier (*RIB* 620; 2115). See also *conubium* [Phang 2001]

constitutio Antoniniana (no pl.): Universal grant of citizenship to free-born non-citizens in AD 212. Cass. Dio 78.9; *FIRA* 88. See also **civium Romanorum** and *peregrinus* [Goldsworthy 2003]

contarius (m. pl. *contarii*): A soldier equipped with the *contus*. *CIL* VIII, 9291. [Goldsworthy 2003]

contubernalis (f. pl. *contubernales*): Mess-mate. A fellow (infantry) soldier. Tac., *Hist.* 1.23; Veg., *DRM* 2.8; *AE* 1987, 944; *Tab. Vind.* 181. See also **contubernium** and **conturmalis** [Goldsworthy 2003]

contubernium (n. pl. *contubernia*): 1. A sub-unit of eight men, ten of them making up a *centuria*. (Veg., *DRM* 2.8; 2.13; *RIB* 2496.3); 2. used figuratively to refer to the accommodation itself (Tac. *Ann.* 1.41). [Goldsworthy 2003]

conturmalis (m. pl. *conturmales*): Mess-mate or fellow cavalryman. Amm. 16.12.45; *Tab. Vind.* 329.3. See also

turma and ***contubernalis*** [Goldsworthy 2003]

contus (m. pl. *conti*): A two-handed, long cavalry spear or lance. Tac., *Ann.* 6.35; *Hist.* 1.44. Carried by a ***contarius***. [Bishop and Coulston 2006]

conubium (n. pl. *conubia*): The right to contract a legal marriage or *iustum matrimonium*. Soldiers were not permitted to marry whilst serving and one of the rights granted to an auxiliary soldier on a diploma was *conubium*. Gaius 1.57; *RMD* 189. [Phang 2001]

cop(u)la (f. pl. *cop(u)lae*): A grappling hook, as used in naval warfare to hold ships together in combat. Caes., *BG* 3.13.8; *P. Mich.* 8.467.20. [Goldsworthy 2003]

cornicen (m. pl. *cornicines*): A musician who played the *cornu*. Veg., *DRM* 2.22; *AE* 1997, 1628. [Goldsworthy 2003]

cornicularius (m. pl. *corniculari*i): A clerk or secretary (Suet., *Dom.* 17.2; *CIL* VIII, 2739); ***c. legati Augusti***: on the staff of a provincial commander (*CIL* III, 9908); ***c. legati legionis***: on the staff of a legionary commander (*CIL* III, 4363); ***c. tribuni***: on the staff of a military tribune (*CIL* VIII, 18078). [Goldsworthy 2003]

cornu (n. pl. *cornua*): A curving horn, played by the *cornicen*. Used to instruct the *signa*, rather than the men directly. Varro, *LL* 5.16; Tac., *Ann.* 1.68. [Bishop and Coulston 2006]

corona (f. pl. *coronae*): A crown, part of the *dona militaria*, awarded for gallantry (Aul. Gell. 5.6.1); ***c. aurea***: the golden crown, another name for the *c. triumphalis* (Pliny, *NH* 16.3; *CIL* II, 2637); ***c. civica***: the civic crown, made of oak leaves, awarded to a soldier who saved the life of a citizen (Aul. Gell. 5.6.11; Pliny, *NH* 16.3); ***c. civica aurea***: the golden civic crown, another name for the *c. aurea* (*CIL* XI, 7264); ***c. castrensis***: the camp crown, usually of gold, awarded to the first soldier to scale an enemy camp's walls (Aul. Gell. 5.6.17); ***c. graminea***: the grass crown, another name for the *c. obsidionalis* (Pliny, *NH* 22.4); ***c. muralis***: the mural crown, usually of gold, awarded to the first soldier to scale an enemy city's walls (Aul. Gell. 5.6.16; *CIL* III, 454); ***c. navalis***: the naval crown, usually of gold, awarded to the first man to board an enemy ship in battle (Aul. Gell. 5.6.18; *CIL* X, 8291); ***c. obsidionalis***: the siege crown, awarded to a relieving general by besieged inhabitants (Aul. Gell. 5.6.8; Pliny, *NH* 22.4); ***c. ovalis***: the ovation crown, awarded to a general celebrating an ovation (Aul. Gell. 5.6.20); ***c. triumphalis***: the triumphal crown, made of gold, awarded to a general celebrating a triumph (Aul. Gell. 5.6.5; *CIL* V, 3348); ***c. vallaris***: the rampart crown, another name for the *c. castrensis* (Pliny, *NH* 16.3; *CIL* X, 8291). [Maxfield 1981]

corporis custodes see ***Germani corporis custodes***

corvus (m. pl. *corvi*): Literally 'crow', a device used to fasten two ships together during combat at sea, which took the form of a bridge that rotated about a pole, with a spike (like a crow's beak) beneath the bridge. Curt. 4.2.12; Polyb. 1.22–3. [Goldsworthy 2003]

crista (f. pl. *cristae*): A helmet crest (Livy 10.39.12). ***c. transversa***: a transverse crest worn by the *centurio* (Veg., *DRM* 2.12). [Bishop and Coulston 2006]

cui praeest (Phr.) Literally 'which is commanded by', used to refer to the

The **lorica, vitis, ocreae,** *and* **crista transversa** *of* **centurio** *T. Calidius Severus*

named commander of a (normally auxiliary) unit. *CIL* XVI, 69. [Goldsworthy 2003]

cuneus (m. pl. *cunei*) 1. Literally 'a wedge', a type of formation in that shape used in battle and countered with the *forceps* (Fest. s.v.; Veg., *DRM* 3.19; Aul. Gell. 10.9.1). 2. An irregular auxiliary unit, often mounted (*ND Or.* XXXIX.1–9. *RIB* 882; 1594). See also ***caput porcinum*** and ***forceps*** [Cowan 2007]

curator (m. pl. *curatores*): A *principalis* with a particular responsibility; *c. cohortis*: a *primus pilus* charged with looking after a *cohors* of the *vigiles* (*CIL* VI, 32760); *c. fisci*: with financial responsibilities in the urban and Praetorian cohorts (*CIL* II, 2610); *c. opera armamentarii*: with responsibility for the camp *armamentarium* (*CIL* VIII, 2563); *c. pro praefecto cohortis*: a *subpraefectus* in temporary charge of an auxiliary unit

(*AE* 1895, 36); *c. tabularii legionis*: an *evocatus* in charge of the legionary *tabularium* (*CIL* VIII, 2852); *c. turmae*: supervised the supply of fodder and horses for a *turma* (*CIL* VIII, 2094); *c. veteranorum*: in charge of **veterani** (*CIL* V, 3375; 7005). [Goldsworthy 2003]

cursus honorum (Mod.): The career structure of a senatorial officer. [Goldsworthy 2003]

custos armorum (m. pl. *custodes armorum*): Literally 'keeper of the weapons'. An *immunis* in every *centuria* and *turma* who may be presumed to be associated with the *armamentarium*. *Dig.* 49.16.14; *CIL* V, 5196. See also ***armicustos*** [Goldsworthy 2003]

decanus (m. pl. *decani*): Head of a *contubernium* in the Late Roman period, but under the Principate and Republic no title is associated with the post (although inscriptions do appear to record 'the *contubernium* of', e.g. *AE* 2009, 955 or *CIL* XIII, 11954a). Veg., *DRM* 2.8; *AE* 1951, 30. [Southern and Dixon 1996]

decimatio (m. pl. *decimationes*) Selecting one in ten soldiers for capital punishment. Polyb. 6.38.2–4; Tac., *Ann.* 3.31; *HA*, *Macr.* 12. [Brand 1968]

decurio (m. pl. *decuriones*): Officer in charge of a *turma* of cavalry (Veg., *DRM* 2.14; *CIL* 13, 8094; *AE* 1998, 838); *d. princeps*: Senior *decurio* in a unit (*RIB* 1991; *CIL* VI, 31174). [Goldsworthy 2003]

decursio (m. pl. *decursiones*): A series of military manoeuvres, often associated with *lustratio* in the Republican period. Suet., *Galb.* 6.3; Livy 40.6.5; 44.9.6; Tac., *Ann.* 2.55. See also *campicursio* [Goldsworthy 2003]

depositum (n. pl. *deposita*): In its plural form, referring to the savings of a soldier held by a unit in its strongroom, under the charge of the *signifer.* Veg., *DRM* 2.20; *P. Columbia* inv. 325. [Goldsworthy 2003]

dies natalis aquilae see *natalis aquilae*

dilectus (m pl. *dilectūs*): A levy of troops, traditionally voluntary after the time of Marius and into the Principate. Cic., *Phil.* 11.24; App. 5.17.68; Tac., *Ag.* 7.5. [Goldsworthy 2003]

diploma (Mod.): A copper-alloy copy of a legal document granting rights to a discharged soldier. Most are auxiliary but there are examples from the *cohortes praetoriae*, *equites singulares Augusti*, and fleet members. The originals were normally publicly posted in Rome itself. [Goldsworthy 2003]

discens (part. pl. *discentes*): Trainee (or, in some interpretations, instructor), as in *d. aquilifer(or)um* (*CIL* VIII, 2569; 2988),

d. signifer(or)um (assuming this is the correct expansion of *DS*: *CIL* VIII, 2569), and *d. lanc(h)iariorum* (*AE* 1993, 1575). [Goldsworthy 2003]

disciplina (f. sing.): The quality (sometimes even personification) of military discipline, promoted by the Emperor Hadrian. Invocations of the deity have sometimes been seen as indications of a lack of discipline. Tac., *Ann.* 1.35; *RIB* 1127; 3298. [Goldsworthy 2003]

dolabra (f. pl. *dolabrae*): A mattock or pickaxe. Used as a tool for excavation, it could also in extreme circumstances serve as a weapon. Livy 9.37.8; Tac., *Ann.* 3.46; *AE* 2009, 754; *P. Mich.* 8.467.19–20. [Bishop and Coulston 2006]

domine (Phr.): Form of address to a social or military superior, equivalent to 'sir'. *Tab. Vind.* 175; *AE* 2007, 872. [Goldsworthy 2003]

dona militaria (pl.): System of awards given to Roman soldiers for valour. These included the *corona*, *torques*, *armilla*, *hasta pura*, and *phalerae*. *CIL* III, 550; 6809. [Maxfield 1981]

donativum (n. pl. *donativa* Ang. donative): A one-off cash payment made to members of the army. Ultimately used to purchase the Empire under the Principate. Suet., *Cal.* 46; Tac., *Ann.* 12.41; *HA*, *Pert.* 4.6. [Goldsworthy 2003]

donis donatus (Phr.): Literally 'given awards', used of soldiers awarded for bravery. *CIL* III, 1940; *AE* 1969/70, 583. [Maxfield 1981]

draco (m. pl. *dracones*): A standard in the form of a serpent, with a metallic head and a cloth body that functioned like a

*A **diploma** granting Roman citizenship and the right of* **conubium** *to a member of the* **classis Ravennatis**

windsock. Veg., *DRM* 2.13; Amm. 16.10.7; Arr., *Tech. Takt.* 35.3–4. [Bishop and Coulston 2006]

draconarius (m. pl. *draconarii*): Standard-bearer who carried the *draco*. Veg., *DRM* 2.7; 2.13; Amm. 20.4.18; *AE* 1891, 105. [Goldsworthy 2003]

dromedarius (m. pl. *dromedarii*): A camel rider, apparently attached to a *turma* in eastern provinces. *BGU* 696 1.33; 2.1012. [Goldsworthy 2003]

ducenarius (m. pl. *ducenarii*): A cavalry rank in the Late Roman army, possibly the commander of 200 men. Also a pro-curatorial salary grade. Hier., *CIH* 19; Veg., *DRM* 2.8; *CIL* III, 99; XI, 4787. [Southern and Dixon 1996]

duplarius (m pl. *duplarii*): A *principalis* in a legionary or praetorian *centuria* receiving double pay. Veg., *DRM* 2.7; *AE* 1992, 1307; *CIL* VI, 2461. [Goldsworthy 2003]

duplicarius (m. pl. *duplicarii*): A *principalis* in a *turma* receiving double pay. Equivalent to an *optio* in a *centuria*.

Livy 2.59.11; Caes., *BC* 3.53; *RIB* 201; 2140; *AE* 1969/70, 583. [Goldsworthy 2003]

dux (m. pl. *duces*): A general or army commander (Caes., *BG* 1.13.2; Tac., *Hist.* 3.37); **d. legionum**: Commander of a detachment or vexillation (*CIL* III, 1919; 8513; 12813). [Southern and Dixon 1996]

ephippium (n. pl. *ephippia*): Saddle. Caes., *BG* 4.2.4. See also **scordiscus** and **sella** [Bishop and Coulston 2006]

eques (m. pl. *equites*): 1. A member of the equestrian order, for whom military service in the *tres militiae* formed part of their career structure as *praefectus* and *tribunus* (Suet., *Claud.* 25). 2. An auxiliary cavalryman serving in either a *cohors equitata* or an *ala* (*RIB* 121; 3185); **e. alaris**: a cavalryman in an *ala* (*CIL* VIII, 4800); **e. cohortalis**: a cavalryman in a mixed cohort (*CIL* VIII, 2532); **e. legionis**: a rider in a legion, normally used as messengers under the Principate (Arr., *Ek.* 5; Veg., *DRM* 2.2; *AE* 1913, 48; *RIB* 482); **e. praetorianus**:

a cavalryman in a Praetorian cohort (*CIL* III, 13201); *e. promotus*: in the Late Roman army, a cavalryman in a unit originally detached from legionary cavalry (*CIL* XIII, 6823); *e. singularis Augusti*: a cavalryman in the bodyguard of the emperor, often of Batavian origin (*CIL* VI, 31173; XIV, 2952); likewise *e. singularis imperatoris* (*CIL* VI, 3262). See also *miles* [Goldsworthy 2003; Speidel 1994]

equis(i)o (m. pl. *equis(i)ones*): Stable hand or groom (*CIL* III, 13370); *e. consularis*: army commander's groom (*Tab. Vind.* 310.24) [Goldsworthy 2003]

equitata (adj.): Literally 'on horseback', referring to a part-mounted auxiliary *cohors. DMC* 19; *AE* 1925, 44; *CIL* XIV, 3548. [Goldsworthy 2003]

eunema (Celt.): Throwing javelins at targets from a moving horse, as part of the *hippika gymnasia* (Arr., *Tech. Tak.* 42) [Hyland 1993]

evocatus (m. pl. *evocati*): A soldier recalled after retirement (*CIL* III, 3565); *e. Augusti*: a former Praetorian Guardsman recalled or re-enlisted (*CIL* III, 6359; V, 7160). [Goldsworthy 2003]

exactus (m. pl. *exacti*): A clerk on the staff of an *officium* (*CIL* XIV, 2255; *AE* 1993, 1577); *e. consularis*: a clerk on the staff of an army commander (*CIL* XIII, 6738); *e. exercitus*: clerk serving on the staff of a provincial army (*CIL* VIII, 990); *e. legionis*: a clerk on the staff of a legion (*CIL* VIII, 2956); *e. officii praesidis*: a clerk on the staff of a *praeses* (*CIL* II, 4311). [Goldsworthy 2003]

ex acuminibus (Phr.): Divination from electrical discharges from the tips of weapons. Cic., *Div.* 2.77. [Goldsworthy 2003]

exceptor (m. pl. *exceptores*): a scribe or short-hand writer (*Dig.* 19.2.19); *e. officii praesidis*: scribe in the *officium* of a *praeses* (*CIL* VIII, 17634); *e. tribuni*: scribe of a *tribunus* (*CIL* VI, 1057). [Goldsworthy 2003]

excubiae (f. pl.): Pickets, sentries, or watches. Tac., *Ann.* 13.18; Veg., *DRM* 3.8. [Goldsworthy 2003]

exercitatio (m. pl. *exercitationes*): Exercises or training (Veg., *DRM* 2.23; *CIL* VIII, 2532); *e. equestris* see *hippika gymnasia* [Goldsworthy 2003]

exercitator (m pl. *exercitatores*): Trainer (*CIL* III, 3470); *e. equitum*: horse trainer (*CIL* III, 3395). [Goldsworthy 2003]

exercitologist (pl. **exercitologists** Mod.): One who practices **exercitology**. [Bishop 2014]

exercitology (Mod.): The study (*logia*) of the Roman army or armies (*exercitus*). I made that one up, but that is just one of the many glories of the English language, after all. http://bit.ly/1yN2LU3 [Bishop 2014]

exercitus (m. pl. *exercitūs*): An army (but seldom *the* army: Romans were much more likely to refer to *milites*). Under the Republic, a consular army. Under the Principate, however, this evolved to mean a provincial or regional army, so what is now thought of as The Roman Army was made up of several armies and celebrated as such in an issue of coins by Hadrian (*Dig.* 3.2.2; Livy 26.42.2); *e. Britannicus*: the army of Britannia (Tac., *Hist.* 1.61; *CIL* VI, 3358; XIII, 8805; *RIC* II 912–13, 458); *e. Cappadocicus*: the army of Cappadocia (*RIC* II 914, 458); *e. Dacicus*: the army of Dacia (*RIC* II,915–19a); *e. Delmaticus*: the army of Dalmatia (Tac., *Hist.* 2.11); *e. Germanicus*: the army of Germania

(Tac., *Hist.* 1.19; *AE* 2002, 917; *RIC* II, 920–1, 459;); *e.* **Germanicus Inferior**: the army of Germania Inferior (*AE* 1975, 639e); *e.* **Hispanicus**: the army of Hispania (*RIC* II 922–3, 460); *e.* **Iudaicus**: the army of Judaea (Tac., *Hist.* 1.76); *e.* **Mauretanicus**: the army of Mauretania (*RIC* II 924–5, 460); *e.* **Moesicus**: the army of Moesia (Tac., *Hist.* 3.2; *RIC* II 926, 940); *e.* **Noricus**: the army of Noricum (*RIC* II 927, 461); *e.* **Pannonicus**: the army of Pannonia (Tac., *Hist.* 2.11; 85); *e.* **Raeticus**: the army of Raetia (*RIC* II 928–30, 461); *e.* **Romanus**: the Roman army (Tac., *Hist.* 4.57; 75); *e.* **Syriacus**: the army of Syria (Tac., *Hist.* 2.8; *RIC* II 931–7, 462). [Goldsworthy 2003]

exostra (f. pl. *exostrae* Gk.): Literally 'a stage machine', a bridge used to reach the top of enemy walls from a mobile siege tower. Veg., *DRM* 4.21. See also **sambuca** [Campbell 2003]

explorator (m. pl. *exploratores*): A scout or spy, often used to reconnoitre in advance of a moving field army or beyond frontiers to supply information. Caes., *BG* 1.12.2; *CIL* III, 3254; *AE* 1969/70, 583. [Goldsworthy 2003]

extra vallum tendere (Phr.): Literally 'to set up tents outwith the rampart'. Camping in this way was a group punishment inflicted on units or subunits for an offence such as being routed or losing a *signum*. Livy 10.4.4; Tac., *Ann.* 13.36; Front., *Strat.* 4.1.18. See also **signum** [Goldsworthy 2003]

faber (m. pl. *fabri*) Workman, sometimes (but not exclusively) to be found in a *fabrica*. Dig. 50.6.7; Caes., *BG* 5.11.3; *AE* 2009, 752. See also **fabricensis** [Goldsworthy 2003]

fabrica (f. pl. *fabricae*): A workshop, employed in both repair and production of equipment, integral to the army under the Principate, separately established under the Dominate (Veg., *DRM* 2.11; *DMC* 4; *Tab. Vind.* 862; *ChLA* 10.409); *f.* **arcuaria**: a workshop specialising in bows (*ND Occ.* 9.28); *f.* **ballistaria**: a workshop specialising in artillery (*ND Occ.* 9.33; 38); *f.* **loricaria**: a workshop specialising in armour (*ND Occ.* 9.26; 33); *f.* **sagittaria**: a workshop specialising in arrows (*ND Occ.* 9.24; 32; *CIL* V, 8742); *f.* **scordiscoria**: a workshop specialising in saddles (*ND Occ.* 9.18); *f.* **scutaria**: a workshop specialising in shields (*ND Occ.* 9.24; *Or.* 11.39); *f.* **spatharia**: a workshop specialising in swords (*ND Occ.* 9.26; 36). [Goldsworthy 2003]

fabricensis (m. pl. *fabricenses*): A man working in a *fabrica*. During the Principate, these were usually within military bases, but under the Late Empire they would be in the state *fabricae* that were established. Amm. 31.6.2; *CIL* III, 6; *RIB* 156. See also **faber** and **fabrica** [Goldsworthy 2003]

faenaria (n. pl.): A deduction from the pay of a cavalryman to cover the cost of hay (30 *sestertii* per annum in the 1st century AD). *RMR* 47.1. [Goldsworthy 2003]

falcata (f. pl. *falcatae* Mod.): A curved, single-edge sword from the Iberian peninsula. See also **machaera** [Bishop and Coulston 2006]

falx (f. pl. *falces*): 1. A sickle used for harvesting during foraging expeditions, depicted in use on Trajan's Column (Varro, *RR* 1.50.1); 2. a two-handed, single-bladed sword used by the Dacians (Fronto, *Princ. Hist.* 5); *f.* **muralis**: a

A **falx** *depicted on an iunscription set up at Birdoswald by* Cohors I Aelia Dacorum

weapon used for defending walls during sieges (Caes., *BG* 3.14.5); *f. navalis*: a curved blade used for severing rigging at sea (Caes., *BG* 3.14.5; Veg., *DRM* 4.46). [Bishop and Coulston 2006]

Feriale Duranum (Mod.): A document on papyrus, dating to AD 225–35 and excavated at Dura-Europos, which gives a calendar of religious festivals observed by *cohors XX Palmyrenorum. RMR* 117. [Goldsworthy 2003]

focale (n. pl. *focalia* Mod.): Identified by modern commentators with the neck cloth, cravat, or scarf worn by soldiers, ostensibly to prevent chafing caused by armour. See also *orarium* [Sumner 2009]

focaria (f. pl. *focariae*): A soldier's common-law wife or concubine. *CIL* XI, 39; *AE* 1934, 36; *Pap. Choix* 6.8. [Phang 2001]

foederatus (m. pl. *foederati*): 1. In the Republican or Imperial periods, a member of an allied force provided as part of the terms of a treaty (*foedus*) (Livy 25.18.10; 34.57.9); 2. under the Late Empire, a member of a formation of barbarian troops, from within or outwith the empire, in Roman service because of

a treaty agreement (Amm. 18.2.13; *CIL* VI, 10212). See also *bucellarii* [Southern and Dixon 1996]

forceps (f. pl. *forcipes*): Literally 'pincers', a battlefield formation used to counter the *cuneus* by mirroring its shape (centre held back and flanks advanced). Aul. Gell. 10.9.1. See also *forfex* [Cowan 2007]

forfex (f. pl. *forfices*): Literally 'shears' or 'claw', a battlefield formation used to counter the *cuneus* by mirroring its shape (centre held back and flanks advanced). Fest. s.v.; Veg., *DRM* 3.19. See also *forceps* [Cowan 2007]

forum (n. pl. *fora*): A central open area within a Republican fortification, equivalent to the *principia* courtyard in one of the Principate. Polybios (6.31.1) uses the equivalent Gk. word (ἀγορά, echoed by Jos., *BJ* 3.5.2) in his description of a Republican camp. Livy 41.2.11; Fest. s.v. [Johnson 1983]

fossa (f. pl. *fossae*): A defensive ditch; *f. fastigata*: a symmetrically V-sectioned ditch; *f. Punica*: an asymmetrically V-sectioned ditch. *DMC* 49; *CIL* VIII, 979; 2532. See also *fossatum* [Johnson 1983]

fossatum (n. pl. *fossata*): A defensive

Legionarii *undertaking* **frumentatio** *on Trajan's Column*

Troops with **fustes** *on Trajan's Column*

ditch. Veg., *DRM* 4.16. See also *fossa* [Johnson 2003]

framea (f. pl. *frameae*): A German javelin that also served as a thrusting spear for close combat. Tac., *Ger.* 6; Aul. Gell. 10.25.2. [Bishop and Coulston 2006]

frater (Phr.): Literally 'brother', a form of address used for social and military peers. In some instances difficult to distinguish from a blood relative (e.g. *AE* 2005, 255). *Tab. Vind.* 248; 255. See also *commilito* [Goldsworthy 2003]

frons (f. pl. *frontes*): The front (or frontage) of the battle line, or that part facing the enemy. Livy 5.38.2; Aul. Gell. 10.9.1; Tac., *Hist.* 2.89; Veg., *DRM* 3.14. [Cowan 2007]

frumentarius (m. pl. *frumentarii*): Although beginning as officers responsible for the supply of *frumentum*, the *frumentarii* evolved into couriers attached to the staff of a provincial commander and ultimately internal security agents. Caes., *BG* 8.35.4; *HA*, *Hadr.* 11.4–6; *CIL* III, 6084. [Goldsworthy 2003]

frumentatio (f. pl. *frumentationes*): 1. Foraging, usually whilst on campaign (Caes., *BG* 6.39); 2. grain issue to soldiers (Livy 31.36.5; Suet., *Galb.* 20.2). [Goldsworthy 2003]

frumentum (n. pl. *frumenta*): Grain, corn, or wheat. Livy 23.12.4; Caes., *BG* 1.16. [Goldsworthy 2003]

funda (f. pl. *fundae*): A sling. Caes., *BG* 4.25.1; Livy 38.29.4; Veg., *DRM* 4.22. [Bishop and Coulston 2006]

fundibalator (m. pl. *fundibalatores*): One who uses the *fustibalus*. Veg., *DRM* 3.14. [Goldsworthy 2003]

fundibalus see *fustibalus*

funditor (m. pl. *funditores*): A slinger. Caes., *BG* 2.7.1; Sall., *Iug.* 46.7; Livy 38.29.4. [Goldsworthy 2003]

furca (f. pl. *furcae*): 1. A forked pole for carrying the baggage of a soldier (Front., *Strat.* 4.1.7); 2. A forked pole used for pushing away scaling ladders during a siege (Livy 28 3.7; Caes., *BC* 2.11). See also *muli Mariani* [Goldsworthy 2003]

fustibalus (m. pl. *fustibali*): A staff sling. Veg., *DRM* 3.14. [Bishop and Coulston 2006]

fustis (m. pl. *fustes*): A club or cudgel. Native irregulars are shown armed with these on Trajan's Column, whilst they were used by troops to administer the *fustuarium* form of capital punishment. Tac., *Ann.* 3.21; Vell. Pat. 2.78. See also *fustuarium* [Bishop and Coulston 2006]

fustuarium (n. pl. *fustuaria*): Capital punishment administered with cudgels or clubs by fellow soldiers to the victims. Cic., *Phil.* 3.6.14; *Dig.* 48.19.7. See also *fustis* [Brand 1968]

gaesum (n. pl. *gaesa* Gk.): A type of javelin used by the Celts. Liv. 8.8.5; Caes., *BG* 3.4. [Bishop and Coulston 2006]

galea (f. pl. *galeae*): A helmet. Isidore (*Orig.* 18.14), a late source, says the *galea* was made of leather (contrary to the archaeological evidence). Cic., *Ver.* 2.4.97; Caes., *BG* 2.20. See also *cassis* [Bishop and Coulston 2006]

galearius (m. pl. *galearii*): A soldier's servant. Veg., *DRM* 3.6; *ChLA* 10.409.2.6. [Goldsworthy 2003]

genius (m. pl. *genii*): A tutelary deity; *g. armamentarii*: the *genius* of the *armamentarium* (*AE* 1978, 707; 2004, 1195); *g. canabensius*: the *genius* of the civil settlement (CIL III, 1008); *g. castrorum*: the *genius* of the camp or fortification (*CIL* VIII, 2529; *AE* 2001, 1727); *g. centuriae*: the *genius* of a *centuria*, possibly with its meaning as a barrack (*CIL* III, 4287; *RIB* 447); *g. cohortis*: the *genius* of a cohort (*CIL* III,

5935; *RIB* 1083); *g. horreorum*: deity overseeing the granaries (*CIL* VI, 235; XIII, 7749); *g. legionis*: the *genius* of a particular legion (*RIB* 327; *AE* 1926, 69); *g. praetorii*: the *genius* of the *praetorium* (*RIB* 1075; 1685); *g. signiferorum*: the *genius* of the standard bearers (*RIB* 451; *AE* 1958, 303); *g. tribuniciali*: the *genius* of the tribunes (*AE* 1898, 12). [Goldsworthy 2003]

Germani corporis custodes (pl): The German horseguard founded by Augustus and disbanded by Galba to be replaced by the *equites singulares Augusti*. Suet., *Cal.* 58.3; *Galb.* 12.2; *AE* 1923, 73; *CIL* VI, 4340. [Speidel 1994]

gladiarius (m. pl. *gladiarii*): A sword smith. *CIL* XIII, 11504. [Bishop and Coulston 2006]

gladius (m. pl. *gladii*): A sword or any kind (Caes., *BC* 3.93.1; Tac., *Ann.* 14.36); *g. Hispaniensis* the short sword with a long point characteristic of Republican and early Imperial infantry (Livy 31.34.4; 38.21.13); *g. pugnatorius*: a sword intended for battle (*P. Mich.* 8.467.19). [Bishop and Coulston 2006]

glans (f. pl. *glandes*): A sling shot, either of lead, stone, or baked clay. Some lead examples were cast in the shape of an acorn (a visual pun, since *glans* also means acorn), whilst other, biconical examples could incorporate messages or even insults. Caes., *BG* 5.43.1; Livy 38.20.1. See also *funda* and *fundibalus* [Bishop and Coulston 2006]

globus (m. pl. *globi*): Literally 'a crowd' or even perhaps (given the humorous names used for battlefield formations) 'a dumpling'. A detached formation, free to attack any part of the enemy line. It was

28

countered with a larger *globus*. Fest. s.v.; Veg., *DRM* 3.19; Aul. Gell. 10.9.1. [Cowan 2007]

gradus (m. pl. *gradūs*): 1. A rank; ***g. deiectio***: reduction in rank, a form of punishment (*Dig.* 49.16.3); 2. a step (or half a pace; there were 1,000 paces in a Roman mile); ***g. militaris***: the military step, which consisted of twenty Roman miles (18.4 statute miles or 29.6km) in five hours (3.7mph or 5.9kph) (Veg., *DRM* 1.9); ***g. plenus***: the full step, or forced march, consisting of twenty-four Roman miles (22.1 statute miles or 35.5km) in five hours (4.42mph or 7.1kph) (Veg., *DRM* 1.9); 3. a position or station, often in battle (Tac., *Hist.* 2.35; Livy 34.39.3). [Goldsworthy 2003]

gravis armatura (Phr.): Literally 'heavily armed', used of heavy (or close-order) infantry and cavalry. Veg., *DRM* 2.2; 2.17. [Goldsworthy 2003]

groma (f. pl. *gromae*): 1. A surveying instrument consisting of a staff supporting a crosspiece with four plumb-bobs. 2. The point from which a camp was laid out, named after 1. 3. The name of a quadrifrons arch (or tetrapylon) sometimes erected over 2., at the junction of the *via praetoria* and *via principalis*, and at the entrance to the *principia*. *DMC* 12; *AE* 1974, 723. [Johnson 1983]

gubernator (m. pl. *gubernatores*): Pilot or helmsman of a ship. *Dig.* 50.6.7; *RIB* 653; *CIL* X, 3432. [Goldsworthy 2003]

habitus (m. pl. *habitūs* Mod.): A military demeanour, as marked by bearing, behaviour, and dress. Apul., *Met.* 9.39. [Phang 2008]

harpago (m. pl. *harpagones* Gk.): A grappling iron, used in siege and naval warfare. Caes., *BG* 7.81.1; Curt. 4.2.12. [Campbell 2003]

haruspex (m. pl. *haruspices*): One who practises divination from entrails, evidently within officers' personal staffs and not integral to the army until the 3rd century AD. *CIL* III, 14214; VIII, 2567; 2586. [Goldsworthy 2003]

hasta (f. pl. *hastae*): A spear, usually consisting of a spearhead, shaft, and ferrule or butt spike (Aul. Gell. 10.25.2; Livy 31.34.4); ***h. pura***: a silver spear, an award given for valour (Pliny, *NH* 7.29; *CIL* III, 6809; VIII, 8934). [Bishop and Coulston 2006; Maxfield 1981]

hastatus (f. pl. *hastati*): A legionary of the front line of a pre-Marian Republican legion, armed with first a spear, later two *pila* (Livy 8.8.6; Varro, *LL* 5.16; Polyb. 6.23); ***h. posterior***: the sixth centurion in a *cohors*, fifth if the first cohort, but in both cases the left rear (*CIL* III, 1480; VIII, 2555); ***h. prior***: the fifth centurion in a *cohors*, fourth if the first cohort, but in both cases the left front (*CIL* III, 263; *RIB* 341). [Keppie 1984]

hastile (n. pl. *hastilia*): A spear shaft. Livy 21.8.10. [Bishop and Coulston 2006]

hemistrigium (n. pl. *hemistrigia*): The width allotted for a *centuria* in a fortification, 30 Rft (8.88m). *DMC* 1. [Johnson 1983]

hiberna (f. pl.): Winter quarters, identifiable with what are now called 'forts' and 'fortresses'. Veg., *DRM* 2.11. See also ***castra hiberna*** [Johnson 1983]

hibernacula (n. pl.): Structures in a *hiberna*. Sometimes also interpreted as a hybrid camp with sheltered tented accommodation. Livy 5.2.1; Tac., *Ann.* 2.23; *CIL* VIII, 2532. [Johnson 1983]

hippika gymnasia (Gk. ἱππικὰ γυμνάσια): A cavalry training or exercise display, often referred to now as 'cavalry sports'. The term only survives in Arrian but may be a transliteration of the Latin *exercitatio equestris*. Arr., *Tech. Tak.* 33–44. [Hyland 1993]

hodoiporikon (Gk. ὁδοιπορικόν): Literally 'the itinerary (or voyage)', leaping fully armed onto a galloping horse, part of the *hippika gymnasia* (Arr., *Tech. Tak.* 43) [Hyland 1993]

honesta missio (f. pl. *honestae missiones*): An honourable discharge from the army, usually achieved after the prescribed period of service. Citizen troops qualified for *praemia militiae*, whilst *peregrini* such as members of the *auxilia* received Roman citizenship. Even those dismissed for *causaria missio* seem to have qualified for *honesta missio*. *Dig.* 49.16.13; *AE* 1961, 169; *CIL* XVI, 69; VI, 3373. See also *causaria missio* and *ignominiosa missio* [Brand 1968]

honori aquilae (Phr.): Literally 'for the honour of the eagle'. This was a phrase marking the 'birthday of the eagle' and thus the foundation of the legion. *CIL* XIII, 6690; 6752. See also *aquila* and *natalis aquilae* [Goldsworthy 2003]

horologiarius (m. pl. *horologiarii*): The keeper of the *horologium*. *CIL* III, 1070. [Goldsworthy 2003]

horologium (n. pl. *horologia*): A timepiece. Pliny, *NH* 7.60; *CIL* XIII, 7800. See also *clepsydra* [Johnson 1983]

horreum (n. pl. *horrea*): A granary or store building. Caes., *BC* 3.42.3; Tac., *Ag.* 19.4; *RIB* 1151. [Johnson 1983]

ignominiosa missio (f. pl. *ignominiosae missiones*): A dishonourable discharge from military service. *Dig.* 49.16.13. See also *causaria missio* and *honesta missio* [Brand 1968]

imaginarius (m. pl. *imaginarii*): A standard bearer who carried the *imago*. Veg., *DRM* 2.7. See also *imaginifer* [Goldsworthy 2003]

imaginifer (m. pl. *imaginiferi*): A standard bearer who carried the *imago*. *AE* 1926, 110; *CIL* XIII, 11868. See also *imaginarius* [Goldsworthy 2003]

imago (f. pl. *imagines*): A standard with a depiction of the emperor, carried by one *imaginifer* in every legion or auxiliary unit. Tac., *Hist.* 3.13; Veg., *DRM* 2.6. [Goldsworthy 2003]

immunis (m. pl. *immunes*): Soldier exempted from fatigues. *Dig.* 50.6.7; *CIL* III, 7449. See also *vacatio munerum* and *principalis* [Goldsworthy 2003]

impedimenta (n. pl.): The baggage train that accompanied an army, inevitably slowing it down. Faster marches could be achieved by abandoning the *impedimenta*. Cic., *Mil.* 10.28; Caes., *BG* 1.26.1; Tac., *Ann.* 1.47. [Goldsworthy 2003]

imperator (m. pl. *imperatores*): A victorious general in the Republican period, acclaimed as such by his troops. The acclamation (recognising his *imperium*) might be used as a title and is the root of the English word 'emperor', once Augustus and his successors became the only commanders (with a few notable exceptions, under Augustus and Tiberius) entitled to use the word under the Principate. Caes., *BC* 2.26.1; Cic., *Ad Fam.* 5, 5; Tac., *Ann.* 3.74; *RIB* 897. See also *imperium* [Goldsworthy 2003]

imperium (n. pl. *imperia*): Power granted to an individual over others, such as the command of a general, and extended to the physical area encompassed by that power (hence the English word 'empire'). Suet., *Iul.* 25.1; Hor., *Car.* 3.5.4; Livy 2.1. See also *imperator* and *provincia* [Goldsworthy 2003]

insigne (n. pl. *insignia*): A mark of distinction or identification, including helmet attachments (presumably crests and plumes). Livy 10.7.9; Caes., *BG* 2.21.1. [Bishop and Coulston 2006; Goldsworthy 2003]

interpres (m. pl. *interpretes*): An interpreter or translator. Also found as *interprex*. *CIL* XIII, 8773; *AE* 1951, 103; 2007, +13. [Goldsworthy 2003]

intervallum (n. pl. *intervalla*): Area between the rampart and the internal structures, so including rampart-back structures. Literally 'within the ramparts.' *DMC* 14. [Johnson 1983]

iovis (Phr.): '... of Jupiter'. Part of a motto found on a belt plate. *RIB* 2429.11. [Bishop and Coulston 2006]

iumentum (n, pl. *iumenta*): A pack animal, such as a mule. Caes., *BC* 1.81.7; Livy 21.37.1; *DMC* 1. [Goldsworthy 2003]

ius iurandum (n. pl. *iura iuranda*): The second, binding, stage of the military oath under the early Republic. Caes., *BG* 7.66.7; Livy 22.38.3; Aul. Gell. 16.4.1. [Brand 1968]

kastrum see *castrum*

kopis see *machaera*

laetus (m. pl. *laeti*): In the Late Empire, *laeti* were incomers provided with land in Italy and Gaul in exchange for military service, and status was hereditary. Amm. 20.8.13; 21.13.16; *ND Occ.* 42.33–44. [Southern and Dixon 1996]

lam(i)na (f. pl. *lam(i)nae*): A plate or sheet; 1. a belt plate (Pliny, *NH* 33.58); 2. a plate in armour (Tac., *Hist.* 1.79); *l.*

levisata: a light plate, possibly from armour (*ChLA* 10.409.1.10). [Bishop and Coulston 2006]

lancea (f. pl. *lanceae*): A javelin. Used by both cavalry and light infantry (like a legionary *lanciarius*). Caes., *BG* 8.48; Tac., *Hist.* 1.79; Suet., *Dom.* 10; *P. Mich.* 8.467.19. [Bishop and Coulston 2006]

lanciarius (m. pl. *lanciarii*): Javelineer. Usually a light infantryman or skirmisher. Amm. 21.13.16; *CIL* III, 6194. [Goldsworthy 2003]

latera praetorii (f. pl. *laterae praetorii*): The central range, comprising the *principia* and accompanying structures on the opposite side of the *via principalis* to the *scamnum tribunorum* (and so between the *retentura* and *praetentura*). *DMC* 23. [Johnson 1983]

legatus Augusti pro praetore (m. pl. *legati Augusti pro praetore*): Commander of a provincial army, directly appointed by the Emperor. Nowadays often referred to as 'provincial governor'. *RIB* 730; 1262. [Goldsworthy 2003]

legatus (Augusti) legionis (m. pl. *legati legionum*): Commander of a *legio* under the Principate with senatorial rank. Caes., *BG* 1.52; Tac., *Hist.* 1.7; *CIL* XIV, 155; *AE* 1926, 79. See also *praefectus legionis* [Goldsworthy 2003]

legio (f. pl. *legiones*, Ang. 'legion'): A legion, comprising around 5,000 *legionarii* in nine *cohortes* (II to X) of six *centuriae*, and one (I) of five double-strength *centuriae*. Commanded by a *legatus (Augusti) legionis*, with the *tribunus legionis laticlavius* as his deputy. Third in command was the *praefectus castrorum*, with the *tribuni legionis angusticlavi* under him and the *primus pilus* next. At any one time, there were twenty-five to thirty-three legions in the Imperial period (*c*.125,000 to 165,000 men) (Tac., Ann. 4.5; Cass. Dio 55.23; *CIL* VI, 3492); *l. comitatensis*: a legion in the mobile field army of the Late Roman period (*ND Occ.* 5; *Or.* 7); *l. palatina*: a legion in the units of the Late Roman period (*ND Occ.* 5; *Or.* 5). [Keppie 1984; Goldsworthy 2003]

legionarius (adj.) 1. Legionary, as in 'legionary centurion' or 'legionary cavalryman' (*AE* 1976, 540: *centurio l.*; *CIL* VIII, 3260: *eques l.*). 2. A legionary soldier (where *miles* is assumed to accompany *legionarius*). Tac., *Hist*. 2.66. Note that the term legionnaire only ever refers to a member of the modern French Foreign Legion. [Goldsworthy 2003]

levis armatura (Phr.): Literally 'lightly armed', used of light (or open-order) infantry and cavalry, used for skirmishing. Veg., *DRM* 2.2; Tac., *Ann*. 2.16; *CIL* IX, 3044. [Goldsworthy 2003]

librarius (m. pl. *librarii*): Record-keeper or clerk (Livy 38.55.8); *l. cohortis*: Clerk on the administrative staff of a *cohors* (*CIL* III, 12602; VI, 221); *l. legionis*: Clerk on the administrative staff of a *legio* (*CIL* III, 909; VIII, 2884; *P. Mich*. 8.466.29; Veg., *DRM* 2.7; cf.2.19). [Fink 1971]

libritor (m. pl. *libritores*): Stone-thrower. Tac., *Ann*. 2.20; 13.39. [Goldsworthy 2003]

liburna (f. pl. *liburnae*): A bireme (a warship with two levels of rowers), named after a type of vessel originally used by Illyrian pirates. Tac., *Hist*. 5.23; *CIL* VI, 1063; VIII, 21025. See also *biremis* [Goldsworthy 2003]

lictor (m. pl. *lictores*): attendant of a senatorial officer who carried the *fasces*, a bundle of rods with an axe head, as a sign of rank. Livy 3.36; Cic., *Pis.* 23.55. [Goldsworthy 2003]

lillia (f. pl. *lilliae*): Literally 'lilly'. Obstacle formed from a sharpened stake, sunk into a pit and concealed with brushwood, rows of pits being offset *quincunx* fashion. Caes., *BG* 7.73. [Goldsworthy 2003]

limitaneus (m. pl. *limitanei*): Frontier soldier, inferior in pay and status to *comitatenses* and *palatini*. HA, *Alex. Sev.* 58; Mal., *Chron*. 12.308; *CIL* III, 11924. [Southern and Dixon 1996]

littera commendaticia (f. pl. *litterae commendaticiae*): A letter of recommendation intended to gain position or rank for the bearer. Cic., *Ad Fam*. 5.5.1; *Dig.*, 41.1.65. [Goldsworthy 2003]

lorica (f. pl. *loricae*): 1. Body armour; a cuirass (Cic., *Flac*. 17.41; Livy 5.38.8); *l. hamata*: Literally 'hooked', chain or ring mail (Mod.); *l. hamata squamataque* (Mod.): suggested as an unambiguous name for fine scale and mail armour (cf. Sil. Ital., *Pun*. 5.140–1); *l. plumata*: literally 'feathered', probably a fine scale and possibly on a fine mail base (Justin, *EHP* 41.2); *l. segmentata* (Mod.): ferrous plate armour articulated on underlying leather straps (the name is post-medieval). *l. squamata*: scale armour (Vulg., 1 *Sam.* 17.5); 2. A breastwork or parapet (Caes., *BG* 5.40; Tac., *Hist*. 4.37). See also *pinna* [Bishop and Coulston 2006]

lupus (m. pl. *lupi*): Literally 'a wolf', a kind of grapnel used by defenders to grab a ram during a siege. Veg., *DRM* 4.23. [Campbell 2003]

lustratio (f. pl. *lustrationes*): The ritual

*A **lustratio** depicted on the Bridgeness Distance Slab on the Antonine Wall.*

purification of an army or fleet before battle, sometimes including the sacrifice of a boar, a ram, and a bull (*suovetaurilia*), as depicted on the Bridgeness distance slab from the Antonine Wall. Cass. Dio 47.38; App. 5.96. [Goldsworthy 2003]

machaera (f. pl. *machaerae* Gk.): A curved, single-edged sword from the Iberian peninsula. Sen., *De Ben.* 5.24.3; Suet., *Claud.* 15.2. See also *falcata* [Bishop and Coulston 2006]

magister (m. pl. *magistri*): Literally 'master'; ***m. equitum***: master of horse (or cavalry), one of the replacements for the Praetorian Prefects under Constantine (Amm. 29.3.6); ***m. militum***: master of troops, ultimately replacing the *magistri equitum* and *peditum* in the western Empire (Amm. 31.1.8; *ND Or.* 7; *CIL* VI,

41389); ***m. peditum***: master of foot (or infantry), one of the replacements for the Praetorian Prefects under Constantine (Amm. 28.5.2). [Goldsworthy 2003]

malleolus (m. pl. *malleoli*): Literally 'a little hammer', an incendiary projectile, usually taking the form of an openwork arrow- or *ballista* bolt-head packed with flammable material. Cic., *Catil.* 1.13.32; Amm. 23.4.14; Veg., *DRM* 4.18. [Bishop and Coulston 2006]

manica (f. pl. *manicae*): An articulated armguard made up of overlapping ferrous or copper-alloy plates which always overlapped upwards from the wrist to the shoulder. These were attached to underlying leather straps by means of rivets. Archaeological finds include examples from Carlisle, León, Newstead, and Sarmizegetusa. Armguards are depicted on the metopes of the *Tropaeum Traiani* (Romania) and a tombstone from Mainz (Germany). Juv., *Sat.* 6.255. [Bishop and Coulston 2006]

manipulus (m. pl. *manipuli* Ang. 'maniple'): Literally 'bundle' or 'handful', this was a tactical unit comprising two *centuriae* in the Republican period (although centuries and barrack blocks continued to be paired into Imperial times). Aul. Gell. 16.4.6; Plaut., *Curc.* 585. [Keppie 1984]

manus (m. pl. *manūs*): A grappling iron, used in siege and naval warfare. Caes., *BC* 1.57.2; Curt. 4.2.12. See also ***harpago*** [Campbell 2003]

marching camp (Mod.): A type of **temporary camp** dug every night whilst on the march. [Jones 2012]

martiobarbulus (m. pl. *martiobarbuli*): Literally 'Mars barbs', an alternative name for *plumbata*. The possibility exists that the original term was *mattiobarbuli*, perhaps in reference to the tribe of Mattiaci. *Veg.*, *DRM* 1.17. See also *plumbata* [Bishop and Coulston 2006]

matricula (f. pl. *matriculae*): Unit nominal roll under the Late Empire. Veg., *DRM* 1. 26; 2.2. See also *numerus* [Fink 1971]

matrimonium (n. pl. *matrimonia*): The legal definition of a relationship between a soldier and a woman; *m. iustum*: a legal marriage, which was denied to soldiers until they achieved the *honesta missio* and afterwards only if both parties were Roman citizens (Gaius 5.7; Ulp. 5.10). [Phang 2001]

mattiobarbulus see *martiobarbulus*

medicus (m. pl. *medici*): Medical orderly or physician. *Dig.* 50.6.7; *m. ordinarius*: medic with the rank of a *centurio*. *RIB* 1618; *CIL* XIII, 11979. [Goldsworthy 2003]

mensor (m. pl. *mensores*): Surveyor, responsible for laying out fortifications. *Dig.* 50.6.7; Veg., *DRM* 2.7; *CIL* VIII, 3028; *m. agrarii*: probably responsible for laying out *territorium* (*CIL* VI, 3606) and perhaps to be equated with the *agrimensor* of Amm. 19.11.8; *m. frumenti (numeris)*: Possibly responsible for measuring out grain (*CIL* X, 130; XIII, 7007). See also *metator*. [Goldsworthy 2003]

metator (m. pl. *metatores*): Surveyor, responsible for laying out fortifications. *DMC* 46; Cic., *Phil.* 11.5.12; Front., *Strat.* 2.7.12. See also *mensor*. [Goldsworthy 2003]

miles (m. pl. *milites*): A foot soldier or infantryman (Caes., *BG* 5.10; *RIB* 2181); *m. gregarius*: an ordinary (or common) soldier (Tac., *Hist.* 5.1; Cic., *Planc.* 30.72); *m. praetorianus*: a member of the praetorian guard (Tac., *Hist.* 2.44; *CIL* III, 5606; VI, 2442). In the later Roman period sometimes found as *milix* (e.g. *CIL* VI, 32980). See also *eques* [Goldsworthy 2003]

militavit (3rd pers. s.): 'He served', used on tombstones to indicate length of military service. *RIB* 294; *CIL* XIII, 8060. See also *aeravit* and *stipendiorum* [Goldsworthy 2003]

militia (f. pl. *militiae*): Military service (*CIL* III, 6687); *m. equestris*: the military postings of an equestrian (to both legionary and auxiliary units) (*AE* 1956, 252); *m. prima*: the first military posting for an equestrian as *praefectus* to command a quingenary auxiliary *cohors* (*CIL* XIV, 2947); *m. secunda*: the second military posting for an equestrian as a *tribunus angusticlavius* in a legion (*AE* 2003, 1803; *CIL* VI, 2131); *m. tertia*: the third military posting for an equestrian as *praefectus* of a cavalry *ala* (*AE* 1955, 228); *m. quarta*: a fourth, unusual, military posting for an equestrian to command one of the few milliary auxiliary units (*CIL* XIII, 6814; *AE* 1956, 124). [Goldsworthy 2003]

militiae mutatio (Phr.): A punishment for self-harm through drunkenness or carelessness, whereby the soldier is forced to change services. *Dig.* 49.16.6. [Brand 1968]

milix see *miles*

mil(l)iaria (adj. Ang. milliary): Double strength, literally 'one thousand', applied to an auxiliary *cohors* or *ala*. *DMC* 16; *AE* 1987, 951; *CIL* X, 4873. [Goldsworthy 2003]

missio (f. pl. *missiones*): Discharge (Livy 26.1.8; *Dig.* 49.16.13.3); *m. causaria*: discharge for a reason (such as disability)

*A **mulus** depicted on Trajan's Column.*

(*Dig.* 49.16.13.3); ***m. honesta***: honorable discharge (*Dig.* 49.16.13.3; *AE* 1921, 21; *CIL* XVI, 10); ***m. ignominiosa***: dishonorable discharge (*Dig.* 49.16.13.3). [Brand 1968]

monoxylus (m. pl. *monoxyli* Gk. μονόξυλος): A hollowed out log used to provide small boats for a pontoon bridge. Veg., *DRM* 2.25; 3.7. See also ***pons navalis*** [Goldsworthy 2003]

morning report (Mod.): Document recording the daily status of a unit. *Tab. Vind.* 154. [Fink 1971]

mucro (m. pl. *mucrones*): The tip of a blade, particularly of a sword. Caes., *BH* 32; Cic., *Phil.* 14.3. [Bishop and Coulston 2006]

mulus (m. pl. *muli*): Each *contubernium* is usually said to have had a mule to carry their heavier equipment, most notably the tent (*papilio*) (although no Roman source exists for this assertion, it appears to be preserved in Maur., *Strat.* 4.B.22); mules were widely used by the army as pack animals. Caes., *BG* 7.45.2; *HA, Had.* 17.2. See also ***iumentum*** [Goldsworthy 2003]

muli Mariani (Phr.) Literally 'Marius' mules'. A nickname for legionaries coined in the Republican period, in reference to Marius obliging soldiers to carry their possessions when marching in order to shorten the baggage train (part of which was carried by mules). Front., *Strat.* 4.1.7; Plut., *Marius* 13; Fest. s.v.; 148.6. See also ***furca*** [Keppie 1984]

munifex (m. pl. *munifices*): A soldier who had to perform (or had not been relieved of) *munera*. The term first appears in the 3rd century AD. Fest. s.v.; Veg. *DRM* 2.7; *CIL* V, 896. [Goldsworthy 2003]

munus (n. pl. *munera*): One of the everyday chores, duties, and fatigues soldiers were expected to perform, and from which they naturally sought exemption. Livy 25.7.4. See also ***immunis*** and ***principalis*** [Goldsworthy 2003]

murex (m. pl. *murices*): Named after the spiny shellfish, a metal caltrop consisting of four spikes, one of which always points upwards. Curt. 4.13.36; Val. Max. 3.7.2. See also ***tribulus*** [Bishop and Coulston 2006]

murus (m. pl. *muri*): A defensive stone wall (*CIL* VIII, 2532; *RIB* 1234). See also ***vallum*** [Johnson 1983]

musculus (m. pl. *musculi*): Literally 'little mouse', 'mussel', or 'muscle'. A mobile shed or mantlet used to protect soldiers undermining enemy defences. Veg., *DRM* 4.16; Caes., *BG* 7.84.1. [Campbell 2003]

natalis aquilae (Phr.): Literally 'the birthday of the eagle', marking the day a legion was founded. *CIL* II, 2554; 6183; *AE* 1967, 229. See also ***aquila*** and ***honori aquilae*** [Goldsworthy 2003]

naupegus (m. pl. *naupegi*): Shipwright. *Dig.* 50.6.7; *CIL* XIII, 11861. [Goldsworthy 2003]

nauta (m. pl. *nautae*): Sailor in a *classis*. Caes., *BG* 3.9.1; *CIL* X, 3368. [Goldsworthy 2003]

noverca (f. pl. *novercae*): Literally 'step-mother'. Any part of a *castra* that is poorly sited, normally avoided. *DMC* 57. [Johnson 1983]

numerus (m. pl. *numeri*): 1. A general term for a unit of any kind (Suet., *Vesp.* 6; Tac., *Ag.* 18). 2. An irregular unit (*CIL* VIII, 18026; *ND Occ.* 40.6). 3. Unit nominal roll under the Principate (*Dig.* 29.1.42; *RMR* 87.5). See also **matricula.** [Southern and Dixon 1996]

ob virtutem appellata (adj.): Literally 'so named out of valour', an honorary title given to an auxiliary unit. *RIB* 897; 3298. [Maxfield 1981]

ocrea (f. pl. *ocreae*): The greave; metallic protection for the lower leg. Veg., *DRM* 1.20; Livy 9.40; *HA, Sev. Alex.* 40.5. [Bishop and Coulston 2006]

officialis (m. pl. *officiales*): A member of staff in an *officium*. *AE* 1987, 796. [Fink 1971]

officina (f. pl. *officinae*): Military workshop or works depot, usually manufacturing items such as pottery, tiles, or weaponry. *AE* 1949, 147; Caes., *BG* 1.34.5. [Goldsworthy 2003]

officium (n. pl. *officia*): Office or administrative organisation of a unit. *o. consularis*: office staff of a provincial *legatus Augusti pro praetore* (*CIL* III, 10505); *o. corniculariorum*: office staff under a *cornicularius* (*CIL* VIII, 1875); *o. legati legionis*: the office staff of a *legatus legionis* (*AE* 1993, 1587); *o. praesidis*: the office staff of a *praeses* (*CIL* III, 4311; V, 8275). [Fink 1971]

omnia vos (Phr.): Literally '...all ... you'. Part of a motto found on a 2nd/3rd

century baldric fitting. *RIB* 2429.9. [Bishop and Coulston 2006]

onager (m. pl. *onagri*): 'Wild ass'. Late Roman, single-armed torsion artillery weapon, so called from its resemblance to the kick of the wild mule. Veg., *DRM* 4.22; Amm. 23.4.4. [Bishop and Coulston 2006]

opera vacantes (pl.): Excused duties. *RMR* 58.2.3. See also **vacatio munerum** [Goldsworthy 2003]

optime maxime con(serva) numerum omnium militantium (Phr.): Literally 'Best and Greatest (i.e. Jupiter), protect all serving in the unit'. Motto on 2nd/3rd century AD baldric fittings. *AE* 1912, 291; *RIB* 2429.7. [Bishop and Coulston 2006]

optio (m. pl. *optiones*): Deputy to the *centurio*, elected by the soldiers of a *centuria* (Veg., *DRM* 2.7. *RIB* 492); *o. ad spem ordinis*: An *o.* marked for promotion to *centurio* and awaiting a vacancy (*CIL* III, 12411; *RIB* 544); *o. carceris*: *o.* in charge of prison in Rome (*CIL* VI, 2406; *AE* 1914, 253); *o. custodiarum*: an *o.* in charge of guards (*CIL* XIII, 6739); *o. speculatorum*: an *o.* in charge of *speculatores* (*AE* 1898, 91); *o. valetudinarii*: officer in charge of a *valetudinarium*. (*Dig.*50.6.7; *CIL* IX, 1617). [Goldsworthy 2003]

orarium (n. pl. *oraria*): A scarf worn around the neck by a *tiro* in the imperial *schola*, and possibly other soldiers too. *Pap. Bod.* 29. See also **focale** [Sumner 2009]

orbis (m. pl. *orbes*): Literally 'a ring', a circular battlefield formation, also used for protection for the baggage train and standards when constructing fortifications. Aul. Gell. 10.9.1; Caes., *BG* 5.33.3; Tac., *Ann.* 2.11; Veg., *DRM* 3.8. See also **globus** [Cowan 2007]

A reconstructed **papilio** *for accommodation* **sub pellibus**.

ordinarius (m. pl. *ordinarii*): A *centurio*, the term becoming prevalent in the 3rd century AD. *CIL* V, 8275; XI, 4787; *AE* 1926, 146; *HA, Clod. Alb.* 11.6; Veg., *DRM* 2.7. See also ***ordinatus*** [Fink 1971]

ordinatus (m. pl. *ordinati*): A *centurio*. The term becomes more dominant than *centurio* in the 3rd century. *CIL* VI, 3603; *AE* 1990, 896. See also ***ordinarius*** [Fink 1971]

ordo (m. pl. *ordines*): 1. A rank of soldiers (Sall., *Iug.* 97.5; Caes., *BC* 2.26.4); 2. a unit of men (Caes., *BC* 1.13.4). [Cowan 2007]

ornamenta triumphalia (n. pl.): The dress and trappings worn at a triumph, often awarded in lieu of a triumph itself under the Principate. Tac., *Ag.* 40.1; Suet., *Tib.* 9.2; *CIL* III, 2830; VI, 1444. [Maxfield 1981]

paenula (f. pl. *paenulae*): A woollen cape with a central opening which fastened down the front with buttons or toggles, resembling a poncho. The sides were often rolled or folded onto the shoulders to leave the arms free. It was most popular amongst soldiers in the 1st and 2nd centuries AD. Suet., *Galb.* 6.2; Sen., *De Ben.* 5.24.2; *Tab.*

Vind. 196. [Sumner 2009]

paludamentum (n. pl. *paludamenta*): A type of cloak worn by officers, fastened on the right shoulder, then draped around the neck and over the left arm. According to Pliny, it was dyed red (using the *Kermes* scale insect). Livy 25.16.21; Pliny, *NH* 22.3. [Sumner 2009]

palus (m. pl. *pali*): Stake against which soldiers and gladiators practised sword drill. Veg., *DRM* 1.11; 2.23; Sen., *Epist.* 18.8. See also ***sudis*** [Goldsworthy 2003]

papilio (m. pl. *papiliones*): The *contubernium* tent (referring – it is presumed – to the similarity between a rolled leather tent and the pupa case of a butterfly's larval stage and, spread out, to a butterfly). Usually equated with the rear room of a barrack room-pair (*DMC* 1; *HA, Sev. Alex.* 61). See also ***sub pellibus*** [Goldsworthy 2003]

parazonium (n. pl. *parazonia* Gk. παραζώνιον): A short sword or dagger worn by an officer, usually depicted as having an eagle-headed hilt. Mart. 14.32. [Bishop and Coulston 2006]

parma (f. pl. *parmae*): Small round shield used by the *velites* (Livy 31.35.6); ***p.***

equestris: small round shield used by cavalry (Sall., *Hist.* 4.4; Livy 2.20.10; 26.4.4). [Bishop and Coulston 2006]

patera (f. pl. *paterae* Mod.): A skillet or handled pan in two main forms, both excavated from Roman military sites of the Principate. The first had a flat handle, the second was cast in the shape of a ram's head, an example of the former bearing the stamp of *ala I Thracum* (*RIB* 2415.39). See also *trulla* [Goldsworthy 2003]

pectorale (n. pl. *pectorala*): A small breastplate, worn by the *hastati* in the Republican legion. Varro, *LL* 5.116; Pliny, *NH* 34.43; Polyb. 6.23.14. [Bishop and Coulston 2006]

pecuarius/pequarius (m. pl. *pecuarii*): An *immunis* responsible for looking after cattle or livestock in general. *CIL* III, 11017; XIII, 8287. [Goldsworthy 2003]

peculium castrense (n. pl. *peculia castrensia*): Property owned by the soldier whilst in military service. *Dig.* 49.17; Veg., *DRM* 2.20. [Brand 1968]

pecuniaria multa (Phr.): Fines imposed as punishments for misdemeanours. *Dig.* 49.16.3. [Brand 1968]

peditata (adj.): Literally 'on foot', referring to infantry when applied to an auxiliary *cohors*. *DMC* 4; *AE* 1972, 226. [Goldsworthy 2003]

pedites cohortales (Phr. Mod.): Infantry from auxiliary cohorts. [Goldsworthy 2003]

pelta (f. pl. *peltae*): 1. A crescentic device used in decoration, particularly popular on military inscriptions during the 2nd century AD (Mod.); 2. a type of crescentic shield, used by light infantry, specifically peltasts (Livy 28.5.11). [Bishop and Coulston 2006]

peregrinus (m. pl. *peregrini*): A provincial without Roman citizenship, as were most members of the *auxilia*. Those with peregrine status who served in auxiliary units were specifically granted Roman citizenship in the documents now known as diplomas. Tac., *Hist.* 2.21; *FIRA* 88. See also **diploma** and *constitutio Antoniniana* [Goldsworthy 2003]

per scamnum (adj.): Aligned parallel with the *via principalis*. Inferred from *DMC* 15. [Johnson 1983]

persona (f. pl. *personae*): A face mask, as found on cavalry sports and *clibanarius* helmets. Amm. 16.10.8. [Goldsworthy 2003]

per strigas (adj.): Aligned parallel with the *via praetoria*. Inferred from *DMC* 15. [Johnson 1983]

petrinos (Celt.) The second stage of the *hippika gymnasia*, whereby those attacking the *testudo* are in turn attacked with missiles by the defenders (Arr., *Tech. Tak.* 37) [Hyland 1993]

phalangarius (m. pl. *phalangarii* Gk. φάλαγγαρης): The term *phalangarius* had evidently come into use by the 3rd century AD to distinguish heavy legionaries from *lancearii*. *HA*, *Alex. Sev.* 50.5. See *discens phalangarius* [Goldsworthy 2003]

phalera (f. pl. *phalerae*): 1. A metal disc which formed a junction as part of horse harness (Livy 44.26.6); 2. a metal disc given as an award, part of the *dona militaria* (*CIL* VIII, 217; III, 454). [Maxfield 1981]

pil(l)eus Pannonicus (m. pl. *pil(l)ei Pannonici*): A form of round, fur cap with a flat top worn by soldiers in the Later Roman period even when not wearing helmets and possibly as a helmet liner.

Phalerae *on the horse harness of* **eques** *Romanius from Mainz.*

Frequently worn by *augusti* and *caesares* of the Late Empire, probably to signify their military prowess. Veg., *DRM* 1.20. See also *cento* [Sumner 2009]

pilum (n. pl. *pila*): A heavy javelin consisting of a wooden shaft and a ferrous shank, most having a head designed to pierce both shield and armour, and with both heavy and light and socketed and tanged varieties (Livy 21.8.10; Tac., *Ann.* 2.14; Veg., *DRM* 2.15); *p. muralis*: a type of *pilum* designed for use in defending a rampart (Caes., *BG* 5.40.6; Tac., *Ann.* 4.51); *p. praepilatum*: a *pilum* with a blunted tip, possibly used for training purposes (*Bell. Afr.* 72). [Bishop and Coulston 2006]

pilus (m. pl. *pili*): *centurio* from the right flank of a *cohors*; *p. posterior*: the second *centurio* in a *cohors*, in the right rear (*AE* 1993, 1584; *CIL* VI, 3404); *p. prior*: the first *centurio* in a *cohors*, in the right front (*AE* 1993, 1575; *CIL* III, 6611). See also *primus pilus* [Goldsworthy 2003]

pinna (f. pl. *pinnae*): Literally 'a fin', a merlon on top of a breastwork. Caes., *BG* 5.40; Aul. Gel. 9.1.1. See also *lorica* [Goldsworthy 2003]

plumbata (f. pl. *plumbatae*): A dart weighted with lead (Veg., *DRM* 1.17); *p. tribolata*: a spiked version of the missile (*DRB* 10). See also *martiobarbulus* [Bishop and Coulston 2006]

pluteus (m. pl. *plutei*): 1. A mantlet or mobile shed (a three-wheeler, according to Vegetius, arched and formed of wicker), used to protect besiegers attacking a fortification (Caes., *BC* 2.9.2; Veg., *DRM* 4.15; Amm. 21.12.6); 2. A breastwork or parapet (Caes., *BG* 7.41; *BC* 3.24). See also *propugnaculum* [Campbell 2003]

pons navalis (m. pl. *pontes navales*): A pontoon bridge, constructed from a series of boats joined together with a roadway. Amm. 17.12.4; 18.7.2. See also *monoxylus* [Goldsworthy 2003]

porta (f. pl. *portae*): Gate or gateway in a fortification (*CIL* III, 368; *RIB* 1234); *p. decumana*: the gate on the *via decumana*, in the *retentura* (*DMC* 18); *p. praetoria*: The gate on the *via praetoria* immediately in front of the *principia*, in

the *praetentura* (*DMC* 3; *CIL* III, 7450);
p. principalis dextra: the gate on the *via principalis* to the right of the *principia*, when standing at the *groma*, facing the *porta praetoria* (*DMC* 14); **p. principalis sinistra**: the gate on the *via principalis* to the left of the *principia*, when standing at the *groma*, facing the *porta praetoria*. (*DMC* 14). [Johnson 1983]

posca (f. no pl.): A mixture of vinegar and water drunk by legionaries as field rations. App. 9.54; *HA*, *Hadr*. 10. [Goldsworthy 2003]

postsignanus (m. pl. *postsignani*): Literally 'behind the standards', troops stationed behind the standards. Amm. 18.8.7; 24.6.9; *BCTH* 1905, 243 [Goldsworthy 2003]

praefectus (m. pl. *praefecti*): an equestrian officer; **p. Aegypti**: commander of the Egyptian army (Suet., *Vesp*. 6.3; *CIL* XI, 7285); **p. alae**: commander of an *ala* (Tac., *Hist*. 2.59; *CIL* XIII, 8842; see also *p. equitum*); **p. castrorum**: third highest-ranking officer in a *legio*, with logistical responsibilities (Veg., *DRM* 2.10; Vell. Pat. 2.119; *CIL* III, 8472); **p. classis**: commanding officer of a fleet (Tac., *Hist*. 3.12; *CIL* II, 1267); **p. cohortis**: commander of an auxiliary *cohors* (Sall., *Iug*. 46.7; *AE* 1988, 185); **p. equitum**: commander of an *ala* (Caes., *BG* 8.12.4; *AE* 1978, 583; see also *p. alae*); **p. fabrum**: Early Republican-period officer in charge of engineering, later a general's aide-de-camp, but by the Principate just an honorary title (Caes., *BC* 1.24.4; *CIL* X, 4872); **p. laetorum**: in the Late Empire, the commander of a unit of *laeti* (*ND Occ*. 42.33–44); **p. legionis**: the commander of a *legio* in Egypt, after Severus in

Mesopotamia too, and then after Gallienus throughout the empire (Tac., *Hist*. 1.82; *CIL* III, 14137; 6194); **p. numeri**: commander of a *numerus* (CIL XIII, 11979); **p. praetorio**: one of two commanders of the Praetorian Guard (*cohortes praetoriae*) (Suet., *Aug*. 49; Tac., *Hist*. 1.19; *CIL* III, 3258); **p. urbi**: commander of the urban cohorts (*cohortes urbanae*) (Tac., *Ann*. 6.10; *CIL* VI, 1158); **p. vexillariorum**: commander of a detachment (*AE* 1903, 368; *CIL* II, 3272); **p. vigilum**: commander of the *vigiles* (*Dig*. 1.15.3; *CIL* VI, 40840). See also **legatus legionis** [Goldsworthy 2003]

praeiuratio (m. pl. *praeiurationes*): In the Republican period, according to Polybius, as the first stage in taking the oath, an officer read it out, each man then affirming it with the formula '*idem in me*' ('same for me'). Festus called this first part the *praeiuratio*. Polybius, *Hist*. 6.21.1–3. Festus 250L. See also **sacramentum** [Goldsworthy 2003]

praemia militiae (n. pl.): The cash or land grant given to citizen soldiers upon discharge. Aug., *RG* 3; Ov., *Amor*. 1.15.4. [Goldsworthy 2003]

praepositus (m. pl. *praepositi*): An ad hoc commander of a unit of detachment. Tac., *Hist*. 1.36; *CIL* VIII, 3; 21720. [Goldsworthy 2003]

praesentalis (m. pl. *praesentales*): In the Late Roman army, a soldier who attended the emperor or belonged to an eastern field army close to the emperor's presence. *Cod. Just*. 12.54.4. [Southern and Dixon 1996]

praeses (m. pl. *praesides*): Late Roman term for senatorial army commanders and provincial governors. *ND Occ*. 23;

primus pilus	princeps posterior	hastatus posterior
	princeps prior	hastatus prior

Diagram illustrating the **primi ordines** *of a* **legio.**

AE 1980, 793a; *CIL* VIII, 11763.
[Southern and Dixon 1996]
praesidiarius (m. pl. *praesidiarii*): A
soldier left behind in garrison. Livy
29.8.7; Fest. s.v. [Goldsworthy 2003]
praesidium (n. pl. *praesidia*): A garrison
post, used of either the structure or the
troops within. Varro, *LL* 5.90; Sal., *Iug.*
23; Tac., *Ann.* 1.56; *AE* 1927, 49.
[Goldsworthy 2003]
praetentura (f. pl. *praetenturae*): Literally
'the front tented area' on the opposite
side of the *via principalis* to the
principia. DMC 3. [Johnson 1983]
praetorianus (m. pl. *praetoriani*): A
member of the praetorian guard. Tac.,
Ann. 6.3; *Hist.* 1.74. See also **miles
praetorianus** [Goldsworthy 2003]
praetorium (n. pl. *praetoriae*): The
commanding officer's house (but the
combined headquarters area of a
campaign camp). Livy 41.2.11; *DMC* 3;
AE 1964, 148. [Johnson 1983]
prata legionis (n. pl. n/a): Agricultural
land belonging to a legionary base. *CIL*
III, 13250. See also **territorium** [Johnson
1983]
pridianum (n. pl. *pridiana*): An annual (or,
in Egypt, biannual) strength report
detailing additions, losses, and the total
number of troops in a unit. *RMR* 64.
[Goldsworthy 2003]
primus ordo (m. pl. *primi ordines*): One of
the centurions of the first cohort in a

legion. The *primi ordines* consisted of
*hastatus posterior, princeps posterior,
hastatus prior, princeps prior,* and *primus
pilus* in ascending order. *CIL* VIII, 2532;
X, 4872. [Goldsworthy 2003]
primus pilus (m. pl. *primi pili*): The senior
centurion in a legion, commanding the
first *centuria* in the first *cohors*, a position
which potentially opened the way to an
equestrian career (Livy 42.34.11; Caes.,
BC 3.91.1; Veg., *DRM* 2.8; *CIL* II, 1267;
X, 5829); *p. p. iterum*: a member of the
primi pili awaiting appointment to a
tribunate (*CIL* V, 867). See also **primus
ordo** [Goldsworthy 2003]
princeps (m. pl. *principes*): 1. A member
of the second line of the pre-Marian
Republican *legio* (Livy 8.8; Polyb. 6.23),
equipped in a similar fashion to the
hastatus; 2. senior *centurio* in an
auxiliary unit (*RIB* 1982–3); *p.
castrorum*: a senior *centurio* in the
castra praetoria or **castra peregrinorum**
(*CIL* VI, 354; XI, 7093a); *p. posterior*:
the fourth *centurio* in a legionary *cohors*,
third if the first cohort, but in both cases
the centre rear (*CIL* III, 2883); *p.
praetorii*: *centurio* in charge of an army
commander's staff or *officium* (*AE* 1933,
57); *p. prior*: the third *centurio* in a
legionary *cohors*, second if the first
cohort, but in both cases the centre front
(*CIL* XI, 5992; *AE* 2006, 1480).
[Goldsworthy 2003]

principalis (m. pl. *principales*). A junior officer in a *centuria*, such as the *signifer* and *optio*. Vegetius equated *principales* with *immunes*. *AE* 1965, 18; Veg., *DRM* 2.7. [Goldsworthy 2003]

principia (n. pl.): Headquarters in permanent fortifications. A central structure containing the standards. Livy 28.24.10; Tac., *Hist.* 3.13; *RIB* 1092. See also *aedes* and *sacellum* [Johnson 1983]

probatio (f. pl. *probationes* Mod.): The examination of a new recruit, whereby his legal status and eligibility were verified and a physical examination carried out. If successful, a certificate was then issued by the office of the provincial governor concerned and the recruit given a *viaticum* and despatched to a unit. Potential cavalry horses evidently underwent a similar process. The term is inferred from the use of the phrase *probatum/-os a me* by the certifying officer. *RMR* 83; 87; 99; 100. [Goldsworthy 2003]

profectio (f. pl. *profectiones*): Ceremonial departure on a military expedition, under the Republic of consuls, under the Empire of the emperor. Cic., *Sull.* 25.70; Livy 38.44.9; *RIC* 297 var. [Goldsworthy 2003]

propugnaculum (n. pl. *propugnacula*): A breastwork or parapet. Tac., *Hist.* 2.19; *CIL* VIII, 22768. See also *pluteus* [Johnson 1983]

pseudocomitatensis (m. pl. *pseudocomitatenses*): A member of a unit raised from the *limitanei* in support of (but of lower status than) the Late Roman field army *comitatenses*. *ND Oc.* 5.256; *Or.* 7.48; *Cod. Th.* 7.1.18. [Southern and Dixon 1996]

pteruges see *pteryx*

pterygoma (n. pl. *pterygomata* Gk.

πτερύγωμα): Literally a 'wing', a triangular-sectioned wooden strip on either side of the channel of a *ballista*. Vitr. 10.11.7. [Bishop and Coulston 2006]

pteryx (f. pl. *pteryges* Gk πτέρυξ): Literally, a 'feather'; one of a series of strips that fringed the arm holes and lower edge of a cuirass, generally attached to an arming doublet or *sub-armalis*. The word does not occur in Roman sources but has been borrowed from the Greek by modern writers. Xen., *Anab.* 4.7.15; *Peri Hipp.* 12.4. [Bishop and Coulston 2006]

pugio (n. pl. *pugiones*) A dagger. This was carried in addition to the sword by both legionaries and auxiliaries under the Early Empire. Suet., *Iul.* 82.2; Tac., *Hist.* 4.29; *ChLA* 45.1340. [Bishop and Coulston 2006]

pugna publica (f. pl. *pugnae publicae*): Open battle. Veg., *DRM* 3.17. [Cowan 2007]

quaestionarius (m. pl. *quaestionarii*): An interrogator. *CIL* II 4156; VIII, 2751. [Goldsworthy 2003]

quaestor (m. pl. *quaestores*): Officer in charge of provisioning, paying, and recruiting an army in the Republican period. Livy 26.47.8; 40.41.8. [Goldsworthy 2003]

quaestorium (n. pl. *quaestoria*) The accommodation of the *quaestor*, in the Republican period, placed next to the *praetorium*. Under the Principate, still the location where booty, prisoners, and hostages were kept in a campaign camp; in the *quintana* or *retentura*, immediately behind the *principia*. Livy 10.32.8; 41.2.11; *DMC* 18. [Jones 2012]

quartum stipendium (Phr.): Fourth pay period, added by Domitian. Suet., *Dom.*

The **aedes** *or* **sacellum** *of the* **principia** *in the Camp of Diocletian at Palmyra (Syria).*

7. [Goldsworthy 2003]

quincunx (adj.): Something, whether men or pitfalls, arranged in an offset to resemble five spots on a die. Caes., *BG* 7.73.5. See also *cippus* [Goldsworthy 2003]

quingenaria (adj. Ang. quingenary): Normal strength, literally 'five hundred', applied to an auxiliary *cohors* or *ala*. *DMC* 4. [Goldsworthy 2003]

quintana (f. pl. *quintanae*): 1. The *via quintana*, the area behind the *forum* in a Republican camp (Livy 41.2.11); 2. a tax levied on transactions carried out in the camp market (*O. Berenike* 138). See also *via quintana* [Johnson 1983]

quintanensis (m. pl. *quintanenses*): A soldier charged with looking after camp market facilities (reflecting its proximity to the *quintana*). *CIL* XIII, 7749; *O. Berenike* 138. [Goldsworthy 2003]

renuntium (n. pl. *renuntia* Mod.): A document recording that orders had been fulfilled. So called because of the Phraseology beginning '*renuntium* ...'. *Tab Vind.* 134; 143; 574. [Fink 1971]

retentura (f. pl. retenturae): Literally 'the rear tented area', behind the *principia*.

DMC 17. [Johnson 1983]

ripensis (m. pl. *ripenses*): The *ripenses* were units of cavalry and infantry on the river frontiers, consisting of *legiones*, *equites*, *cunei equitum*, and *auxilia*, which included the *cohortes* and *alae*. *Cod. Th.* 7.20.4. [Southern and Dixon 1996]

rorarius (m. pl. *rorarii*): In Livy's description of the early Republican army, these were the younger men who fought behind the *triarii*. Livy 8.8.8. [Keppie 1984]

rosaliae signorum (f. pl.): These were two festivals, recorded in a papyrus from Dura-Europos (known as the *Feriale Duranum*), on May 10 and 31, when the unit *signa* were apparently adorned with wreaths of roses, in an echo of a civil ritual. *RMR* 117. [Goldsworthy 2003]

rostrum (n. pl. *rostra*): the prow of a warship (Caes., *BG* 3.13.8; Livy 28.30.7); *r. trifidum*: a three-pronged prow (Sil. Ital., *Pun.* 6.358). [Goldsworthy 2003]

sacellum (m. pl. *sacella*). Often assumed (on the basis of restored texts *CIL* VIII, 2741 and 18126) to be the shrine of the standards, in the centre of the rear range of rooms in the *principia*. It was normally placed so that there was direct line of site through the *porta praetoria* and the entrance to the *principia* to the standards. *AE* 2007, 1070. See also *aedes* [Johnson 1983]

sacerdos (f. pl. *sacerdotes*): Priest. *RIB* 1314; *RMR* 50. [Goldsworthy 2003]

sacramentum (n. pl. *sacramenta*): The first part of the oath taken by soldiers. Cic., *Off.* 1.36; Liv. 22.38.3; Veg., *DRM* 2.3. See also *praeiuratio* [Goldsworthy 2003]

sagitta (f. pl. *sagittae*): An arrow. Caes., *BG* 4.25.1; Tac. *Ann.* 1.56; Amm. 18.8.11. [Bishop and Coulston 2006]

sagittarius (m. pl. *sagittarii*): 1. Archer (Caes., *BG* 2.7; *CIL* VIII, 2515). 2. Arrow-maker (*Dig.* 50.6.7). [Bishop and Coulston 2006]

sagum (n. pl. *saga*): 1. Cloak, often fringed, and suggested by Polybios (2.28.7) as Celtic in origin. Wrapped around the left arm, it was used in an emergency as a substitute shield (Caes *BC* 1.75; Livy 10.30.10; *Tab. Vind.* 184). 2. Saddle blanket, often fringed (Veg., *Mul.* 1.42.4). [Sumner 2009]

salarium (n. pl. *salaria*): Pay given to equestrian and senatorial officers. Pliny (*NH* 31.41) speculated that the term derived from a time (unspecified) when Roman soldiers were paid in salt. Pliny, *NH* 34.6; Tac., *Ag.* 42.3. [Goldsworthy 2003]

salutatio militaris (Phr.): The military salute, which may be depicted on the so-called Altar of Domitius Ahenobarbus as a tugged forelock. *Bell. Afr.* 85. [Goldsworthy 2003]

sambuca (f. pl. *sambucae*): Literally, 'a harp', used of a portable drawbridge for storming the defences of a fortification (the ropes letting down the bridge supposedly resembled the strings of the instrument). Vitr. 10.16; Veg., *DRM* 4.21. See also *exostra* [Campbell 2003]

Saturnalicium (n. pl. *Saturnalicia*): The Saturnalia festival of 17th December (*Tab. Vind.* 301); *s. k(astrense)*: A deduction made from pay to cover the cost of the camp Saturnalia (*RMR* 68.2.8). [Goldsworthy 2003]

scala (n. pl.): A scaling ladder used in siege warfare. Tac., *Ann.* 13.39; Veg., *DRM* 4.21. [Campbell 2003]

scamnum (n. pl. *scamna*): Literally 'a bench', a zone within the *praetentura* of a fortification; *s. legati*: where the *legati* were based in a multi-legion camp (*DMC* 15); *s. tribunorum*: where the tribunes were based in a camp (*DMC* 15). [Johnson 1983]

schola (f. pl. *scholae*): 1. the meeting place of a *collegium* (*CIL* VIII, 2603); *s. principalium*: a meeting place of *principales* (*AE* 1996, 1358); 2. a military unit under the Dominate (*AE* 1939, 45); *s. palatinae*: a guard unit established by Constantine that replaced the *equites singulares Augusti* (Amm. 14.7.12). [Southern and Dixon 1996]

scopa (f. pl. *scopae*). Literally 'a [besom-type] broom', a bundle of twigs or straw used as a target by archers and slingers. Vegetius, *DRM* 2.23. [Bishop and Coulston 2006]

scordiscus (m. pl. *scordisci*): Saddle (*AE* 1996, 957; Diocl. 10.2); *s. militaris*: a military saddle (*ZPE* 26.125). See also *ephippium* and *sella* [Bishop and Coulston 2006]

scorpio (m. pl. *scorpiones*): Literally 'a scorpion' (referring to its sting). An artillery weapon, originally referring to a bolt-shooter, later to an onager. Veg., *DRM* 4.22; Amm. 23.4.4; Caes., *BG* 7.25. See also *onager* [Bishop and Coulston 2006]

scutarius (m. pl. *scutarii*): 1. A shield-maker (Plaut., *Ep.* 1.1.35; *Tab. Vind.* 184); 2. bodyguard under the Dominate (*AE* 1959, 196). [Bishop and Coulston 2006]

scutatus (m. pl. *scutati*): Literally 'shielded', used synonymously for heavy troops. Caes., *BC* 1.39.1; Livy 28.2.4. See also *caetratus* [Goldsworthy 2003]

scutum (n. pl. *scuta*): A shield (*CIL* VIII, 2532; XIII, 3592); **s. de viminea**: a double-weight practice shield made of wicker (Veg., *DRM* 1.11); **s. planatum**: a flat shield (*ChLA* 10.409.2.13); **s. publicum**: a battle shield (Veg., *DRM* 1.11); **s. talarium**: an ankle-length shield (*ChLA* 10.409.2.9). [Bishop and Coulston 2006]

secutor (m. pl. *secutores*): assistant to an officer (*RMR* 58.2.7); **s. tribuni**: assistant to a tribune, usually in the Rome cohorts (*CIL* VI, 2659; 2987). [Goldsworthy 2003]

seditio (f. pl. *seditiones*): Mutiny. Caes., *BC* 1.87; Tac., *Ann.* 1.17.1. [Goldsworthy 2003]

sella (f. pl. *sellae*): Saddle. *Cod. Just.* 12.50.12. See also *ephippium* and *scordiscus* [Bishop and Coulston 2006]

semispatha (f. pl. *semispathae*): A short sword formed from a cut-down *spatha*. Veg., *DRM* 2.15–16. [Bishop and Coulston 2006]

semissalis (pl. *semissales*): A post in a Late Roman cavalry unit on one-and-a-half-times pay. Equivalent to a *sesquiplicarius*. Hier., *CIH* 19; *CIL* V, 8739. [Southern and Dixon 1996]

sermo castrensis (Phr. Mod.): the Latin spoken (and written) in the Roman army, and by some writers equated with Vulgate Latin, to be distinguished from Classical Latin. [Goldsworthy 2003]

serra (f. pl. *serrae*): Literally 'a saw', a battlefield formation involving repeated advances and retreats, used to reorganise a front line in disarray. Fest. s.v.; Veg., *DRM* 3.19; Aul. Gell. 10.9.1. [Cowan 2007]

serv[a] (Phr.): ?'keep ...' Part of a motto found on a belt plate. *RIB* 2429.12. [Bishop and Coulston 2006]

sesquiplarius (m. pl. *sesquiplarii*): A man on one-and-a-half-times pay. Veg., *DRM* 2.7. See also *sesquiplicarius* [Goldsworthy 2003]

sesquiplicarius (m. pl. *sesquiplicarii*): A cavalryman on one-and-a-half-times pay, as a *principalis*. Equivalent to a *tesserarius* in an infantry unit. *FIRA* 3.47; *CIL* III, 6627. See also *sesquiplarius* [Goldsworthy 2003]

signa convertere (Phr.): face about (Caes., *BG* 1.25; 2.26); **s. efferre**: march out of the camp (Livy 34.46.9); **s. inferre**: advance (Caes., *BG* 1.25; 2.25; Livy 26.6); **s. referre**: retreat (Ov., *Fast.* 3.136; Caes., *BC* 3.99); **s. vellere**: to march out of camp (Verg., *Georg.* 1.108). See also *ad signa convenire* and *signum* [Goldsworthy 2003]

signifer (m. pl. *signiferi*): The standard bearer in a *centuria* or *turma*. A *principalis*, responsible for the savings of his sub-unit, and receiving additional pay for the post. Veg., *DRM* 1.20; 2.7; *CIL* II, 2610; *RIB* 673. [Goldsworthy 2003]

signum (n. pl. *signa*): A standard belonging to a unit or sub-unit. Used for signalling on the battlefield and kept in the *aedes* of the *principia* when in base. Caes., *BG* 2.25; Sall., *Iug.* 80. [Goldsworthy 2003]

singularis (m pl. *singulares*): A bodyguard (Caes., *BG* 4.26; *AE* 1969/70, 583); *s. consularis*: army commander's bodyguard (*CIL* III, 14693; XIII, 8223); *s. imperatoris*: member of the *equites singulares Augusti* (*CIL* VI, 31156); *s. legati*: bodyguard of a *legatus* (*legionis* or *Augusti pro praetore*) (*Tab. Vind.* 154.5). See also *eques singularis* [Goldsworthy 2003]

socius (m. pl. *socii*): Allied soldier in the Republican period. Sall., *Iug.* 95.1; Livy 40.36.9. [Keppie 1984]

spatha (f. pl. *spathae*): Long sword initially used by cavalry under the Principate, derived from European Iron Age long swords. By the end of the 2nd century AD, also used by infantry. Veg., *DRM* 2.15; Tac. *Ann.* 12.35. [Bishop & Coulson 2006]

specularius (m. pl. *specularii*): Glazier. *Dig.* 50.6.7; *CIL* VI, 7299. [Watson 1969]

speculator (m. pl. *speculatores*): A scout or spy. Caes., *BG* 2.11.2; Tac., *Hist.* 2.73; *RIB* 19; *CIL* XIII, 6721. [Goldsworthy 2003]

spolia (n. pl.): Booty captured from an enemy (Cic., *Off.* 1.18.61); *s. opima*: award rarely given to a general who had killed the enemy commander and stripped him of his armour (Cass. Dio 44.4; Plut., *Marcell.* 8.4). [Goldsworthy 2003]

statio (f. pl. *stationes*): 1. A guard post or outpost (Caes., *BG* 6.42; *AE* 2003, 1531); 2. A guard (Caes., *BG* 5.16; *O. Bu Njem* 28; *AE* 1911, 121). [Goldsworthy 2003]

stationem agens (Phr.): Keeping guard, manning a post. Livy 35.29.12; *AE* 1957, 329; *RMR* 58.2.14. [Goldsworthy 2003]

Tombstone of the **signifer** *L. Duccius Rufinus from York*

stator (m. pl. *statores*): Literally 'arrester', so an *immunis* with a custodial function found both in Rome and in the provinces (Cic., *Fam.* 2.19.2; *AE* 1993, 1593; *CIL* XIII, 8670); *s. Augusti*: attached to the emperor (*CIL* VI, 2545).

stimulus (m. pl. *stimuli*): Literally, 'goad'. Obstacle formed from a stake sunk into the ground with a projecting iron spike. Caes., *BG* 7.73; 82. [Goldsworthy 2003]

stipendiorum (3rd pers. pl.): Literally 'of annual payments', used with a number of years on tombstones to indicate length of military service. *RIB* 156; *CIL* XIII, 8094. See also *aeravit* and *militavit*. [Goldsworthy 2003]

stipendium (n. pl. *stipendia*): Annual pay for soldiers, paid originally in three and later four instalments. Caes., *BC* 1.87; *CIL* XVI, 48. [Goldsworthy 2003]

strator (m. pl. *stratores*): A groom, often attached to the staff of an officer. Amm. 30.5.19; *RIB* 233; *CIL* VIII, 18084. [Goldsworthy 2003]

striga (f. pl. *strigae*) The space occupied within a fortification by two *centuriae*, thus two adjacent *hemistrigia*. *DMC* 1. [Johnson 1983]

subarmalis (n. pl. *subarmales*): Padded garment worn under armour. *HA, Sev.* 6.11; *Aur.* 13.3; *Tab. Vind.* 184; *AE* 1998, 839. See also *thoracomachus* [Bishop and Coulston 2006]

sub cura (Phr.): Under the command of. Usually used of a *legatus Augusti pro praetore*. *RIB* 1147; 3215. [Goldsworthy 2003]

subpaenula (f. pl. *subpaenulae*): A garment worn under the *paenula*. *Tab. Vind.* 196. [Sumner 2009]

sub pellibus (Phr.): Literally 'under hides', the modern equivalent being 'under canvas', applied when troops were camping in tents, which were made of goat skin. Caes., *BG* 3.29.2; Tac., *Ann.* 13.35. See also *papilio* [Goldsworthy 2003]

subpraefectus (m. pl. *subpraefecti*): A deputy *praefectus*; *s. alae*: deputy commander of an *ala* in the early Principate (*ILS* 2704); *s. classis*: deputy commander of a fleet (*CIL* VI, 1643); *s. cohortis*: deputy commander of a *cohors* in the early Principate (*ILS* 2703); *s. vigilum*: deputy commander of the *vigiles* (*CIL* V, 8660). [Goldsworthy 2003]

subsidium (n. pl. *subsidia*): A reserve, used in battle to provide flexible support to the main battle line. Aul. Gell. 9.10.1; Sall., *Iug.* 49.6; Veg., *DRM* 3.17. [Goldsworthy 2003]

sub vexillo (Phr.): Literally 'under the *vexillum*', or whilst on detachment. *AE* 1954, 102; 160. [Goldsworthy 2003]

sub vineam iacere (Phr.): A Roman military joke, literally 'to be thrown under the *vinea*', used of a beating by the *vitis* of a centurion. Fest. s.v. See also *sub vitem proeliari* [Goldsworthy 2003]

sub vitem proeliari (Phr.): Another Roman military joke, literally 'to fight under the *vitis*', used when fighting under the *vinea*. Fest. s.v. See also *sub vineam iacare* [Goldsworthy 2003]

sudis (f. pl. *sudes*): 1. A wooden stake used by soldiers to practice sword drill (Veg., *DRM* 2.23); 2. a stake carried by *legionarii* to fortify a rampart on the march (Veg., *DRM* 1.24). See also *palus* and *vallus* [Goldsworthy 2003]

supernumerarius see *centurio supernumerarius*

symmach(i)arius (m. pl. *symmach(i)arii*): A member of an allied irregular unit. *DMC* 19; 29; 43; *AE* 1935, 12. [Goldsworthy 2003]

tabula ansata (f. pl. *tabulae ansatae* Mod.): Literally a 'plaque with handles'. These panels were usually rectangular with triangular extensions (*ansae*) to either side, often used as a decorative panel around inscriptions. [Goldsworthy 2003]

tabularium (legionis) (n. pl. *tabularia (legionibus)*): Legionary record office. *AE* 1898, 108–9. [Fink 1971]

tegimen (n. pl. *tegmina*): A covering, usually of leather, most commonly found on shields but also archaeologically attested for helmets, and designed to protect equipment when not in battle. Caes., *BG* 2.21 [Bishop and Coulston 2006]

tegimentum see *tegimen*

temporary camp (Mod.) A field fortification with tented accommodation. Used of a range of types of fortification from an overnight marching camp through to an *aestiva*. [Jones 2012]

tentorium (n. pl. *tentoria*): Tentage. Caes., *BG* 8.5.2; Suet., *Tib*. 18.2. [Jones 2012]

territorium (n. pl. *territoria*): Land belonging to a legionary base. *CIL* III, 10489. See also ***prata legionis*** [Johnson 1983]

tessera (f. pl. *tesserae*): The watch word for the day (on a writing tablet), kept by the *tesserarius* in a *centuria*. Veg., *DRM* 2.7. See also ***tesserarius*** [Goldsworthy 2003]

tesserarius (m. pl. *tesserarii*): The keeper of the watch word for the day or *tessera* in a *centuria*. Veg., *DRM* 2.7; Tac., *Hist*. 1.25; *CIL* III, 13665; XIII, 6955. See also ***tessera*** [Goldsworthy 2003]

testamentum (n. pl. *testamenta*): A will. Soldiers were given the right to make their own wills and dispose of their property as they wished, part of which might include provision for a tombstone. *CIL* XIII, 5211; *RIB* 108. see also ***castrense peculium*** and ***bona peculium*** [Brand 1968]

testudo (f. pl. *testudines*): Literally 'tortoise'; 1. A close formation whereby soldiers covered their heads with their shields, leaving no gaps (Livy 34.39.6; Caes., *BG* 2.6.2); 2. a type of wheeled timber shed, covered with hides, used to protect a battering ram (Veg., *DRM* 4.14;

A **testudo** *being used by legionaries to attack a city on Trajan's Column*

Vitr. 10.13.2); 3. a stationary defensive cavalry formation in the primary phase of the *hippika gymnasia*, with the riders facing to the rear and covering their horse's rump (and themselves) with their shield whilst opponents threw javelins at them (Arr., *Tech. Tak*. 43). [Cowan 2007; Hyland 1993]

thoracomachus (m. pl. *thorachomachi*): Padded garment worn under armour and made of felt and leather, according to the only source for this term (which advocates its use instead of armour). It is presumed to be the same item as the *subarmalis* (q.v.). *DRB* 15.1. See also ***subarmalis*** [Bishop and Coulston 2006]

tiro (m. pl. *tirones*): A new recruit. Suet., *Tib*. 42.1; *ChLa* 42.1212; *P. Mich*. 8.471. [Goldsworthy 2003]

titulus (m. pl. *tituli*): 1. Literally 'a title', a short transverse earthwork in front of the gate of a temporary camp (*DMC* 49); 2. 'Little Titus', a nickname for a soldier (Festus s.v.). [Jones 2012]

tolleno (m. pl. *tollenones*): A counterbalanced crane used for depositing besiegers onto the defences of a fortification under attack and by Archimedes to grab Roman ships using a grapple. Livy 24.34.10; Veg., *DRM* 4.21. [Campbell 2003]

toloutegon (Celt.): A component of the *hippika gymnasia* whereby riders defended themselves from attack from the rear with spears and swords (Arr., *Tech. Tak.* 43) [Hyland 1993]

tormentum (n. pl. *tormenta*): Artillery powered by twisted skeins of sinew, rope, or hair. Cic., Tusc. 2.24; Caes., *BG* 2.8.4. [Bishop and Coulston 2006]

torquata (adj.): Literally 'decorated with torcs'. A block award of *torques* to an auxiliary unit. *CIL* III, 5775; *RIB* 957. See also **torques** and **bis torquata** [Maxfield 1981]

torques (m. pl. *torquēs*): A neck-ring, based on Gallic/Celtic models (and probably originally actual, captured examples), awarded for bravery. Livy 44.14.2; Suet., *Aug.* 43; *CIL* VIII, 05209. See also **dona militaria**, **torquata**, and **bis torquata** [Maxfield 1981]

transfuga (f. pl. *transfugae*): A deserter. Tac., *Ann.* 4.73; Suet., *Cal.* 47; *Dig.* 49.15.19.8. [Brand 1968]

trecenarius (m. pl. *trecenarii*): The senior *centurio* in the Praetorians. *CIL* III, 454; VI, 33033. [Goldsworthy 2003]

tres militiae equestres (Mod. pl.): The standard three military posts held by an equestrian officer as part of the **cursus**

honorum (typically *praefectus cohortis*, *tribunus legionis*, and *praefectus alae*, in that order). [Goldsworthy 2003]

tria nomina (Mod. pl.): The three names (*praenomen*, *nomen*, and *cognomen*) of a Roman citizen, typically borne by a legionary. [Goldsworthy 2003]

triarius (m. pl. *triarii*): Third line of legionaries in the pre-Marian Republican system, composed of experienced veterans who acted as a tactical reserve, kneeling behind the *hastati* and *principes*. They were not normally used in battle, hence the expression *ad triarios redire*. Livy 8.8.11; Polyb. 6.23. [Keppie 1984]

tribulus (m. pl. *tribuli*): A four-pointed obstacle designed so that one spike always points upwards. The term was evidently applied to both small metal and large wooden versions of the same basic design: the caltrop. Veg., *DRM* 3.8; 24. See also **murex** [Goldsworthy 2003]

tribunal (n. pl. *tribunales*); Platform at one end of the crosshall of the *principia* or on a *campus*. *DMC* 11; *AE* 1933, 214; Tac., *Ann.* 1.18. [Johnson 1983]

tribunus (m. pl. *tribuni* Ang. 'tribune'): An officer of equestrian or senatorial rank, primarily with the *auxilia* (equestrian) and legions (both senatorial and equestrian) (Veg., *DRM* 2.12; Tac., *Ag.* 5); **t. angusticlavius**: Literally 'narrow stripe' tribune, of equestrian rank; there were five in each legion (Suet., *Otho* 10); **t. cohortis**: equestrian tribune in charge of a *cohors milliaria* (*RIB* 2057; *AE* 1956, 123); **t. laticlavius**: Literally 'broad stripe' tribune, of senatorial rank; second-in-command of a legion (*AE* 1912, 17; *CIL* XIV, 3610); **t. vexillationis**: A tribune in charge of a

The eastern **tribunal** *in the* **principia** *at Dura-Europos (Syria).*

vexillatio (Amm. 25.1.9; *AE* 1995, 653; *CIL* XIV, 3602). [Goldsworthy 2003]

trierarchus (m. pl. *trierarchi*): Commander of a warship (not necessarily a *trieris*) in a *classis*. Tac., *Hist.* 2.16; *CIL* VIII, 21025; XVI, 1. [Goldsworthy 2003]

trieris (f. pl. *trieres*): A trireme (a warship with three levels of rowers). Nep., *Alc.* 4.3; *CIL* VI, 1063. [Goldsworthy 2003]

tropaeum (n. pl. *tropaea*): Trophy, usually consisting at the least of a tree adorned with a cuirass and helmet, but usually also other equipment (Tac., *Ann.* 2.18); *T. Traiani*: a large stone monument at Adamclisi (Romania) set up to commemorate Trajan's victory in the Dacian Wars (after which a nearby town was named) (*CIL* III, 14433). [Goldsworthy 2003]

trulla (f. pl. *trullae* Mod.): The term preferred by some scholars for what had previously been identified as a *patera*. See also **patera** [Goldsworthy 2003]

tunica (f. pl . *tunicae*): The tunic worn by members of the armed forces. Initially short-sleeved or even sleeveless and hemmed above the knee, later tunics (as well as early cavalry tunics) had long sleeves. It is shown on some monuments as being knotted on one shoulder. *Tab. Vind.* 196. [Sumner 2009]

turma (f. pl. *turmae*): Sub-unit of an *ala*, probably consisting of thirty-two men, commanded by a *decurio*. Veg., *DRM* 2.14; *DMC*, 27; *RIB* 2415.68. [Goldsworthy 2003]

turris (f. pl. *turres*): 1. A tower on a fortification (Caes., *BG* 5.40.2; *CIL* III, 11965); 2. a moveable wooden tower used in siege warfare (Veg., *DRM* 4.17; Livy 32.17.16–17); 3. a battlefield formation (Fest. s.v.; Aul. Gell. 10.9.1.). [Johnson 1983]

umbo (m. pl. *umbones*): Shield boss. Livy 9.41.18; Amm. 16.12.37. [Bishop and Coulston 2006]

utere felix (Phr.): literally 'use luckily' (or 'happily'). Motto found on a variety of artefacts, including military equipment. *CIL* XV, 7164.

vacatio munerum (f. pl. n/a). Exemption from fatigues, granted to an *immunis*. *Dig.* 50.6.7; Tac., *Hist.* 1.46. See also **opera vacantes** [Goldsworthy 2003]

vagina (f. pl. *vaginae*): Sheath or scabbard of sword or dagger. Caes., *BG* 5.44.8; Pliny, *NH* 33.58; Tac., *Ann.* 15.54; *ChLA* 45.1340.10. [Bishop and Coulston 2006]

valetudinarium (n. pl. *valetudinaria*): A hospital in both a temporary and permanent camp. *DMC* 4; Veg., *DRM* 2.10; 3.2; *Dig.* 50.6.7; *CIL* 3.14537. [Johnson 1983]

vallum (n. pl. *valla*) A defensive rampart or wall (Hadrian's Wall, built of stone, was referred to as a *vallum*: *ND Occ.* 40; *RIB* 2034, not to be confused with the Vallum, a post-Roman name for the earthwork south of Hadrian's Wall). *DMC* 14; *CIL* III, 11965. [Johnson 1983]

vallus (m. pl. *valli*): A stake carried by a *legionarius* to fortify a rampart on the march (Cic., Tusc. 2.37; Livy 33.6.1). See also *palus* and *sudis* [Johnson 1983]

veles (m. pl. *velites*): A light infantryman and skirmisher belonging to the Middle Republican *legio*. *Velites* were equipped with a helmet, sword, javelins, and *parma* and were attached to all of the *manipuli* of *hastati*, *principes*, and *triarii*. They began a battle by forming in front of the heavier infantry, but once their skirmishing duties were no longer required, they would retreat through the *hastati* who would then close ranks behind them. Liv. 26 4.4; Polyb. 6.22. [Keppie 1984]

vericulum (n. pl. *vericula*): Spear with a fifteen-inch (0.37m) iron shank and a three-and-a-half-foot-long (1.05m) shaft. According to Veg., an earlier version of *verutum*. Veg., *DRM* 2.15. [Bishop and Coulston 2006]

ver(r)utum (n. pl. *veruta*): Spear with a fifteen-inch (0.37m) iron shank and a three-and-a-half-foot-long (1.05m) shaft.. According to Vegetius, a later version of *vericulum*. Veg., *DRM* 2.15; Caes., *BG* 5.44. [Bishop and Coulston 2006]

veterana (adj.): Literally 'old', but when applied to the nomenclature of auxiliary units, thought to indicate seniority, where two units with the same name and number are present in the same province. *AE* 1922, 80; *CIL* XVI, 35. [Goldsworthy 2003]

veteranus (m. pl. *veterani*): A retired soldier, usually a legionary, frequently settled in *colonia*. Liv. 37.20; *AE* 1914, 241; *RIB* 3074. [Goldsworthy 2003]

veterinarius (m. pl. *veterinarii*): Veterinary specialist. *Dig.* 50.6.7. *CIL* III, 11215; *Tab. Vind.* 310. [Goldsworthy 2003]

veterinarium (n. pl. *veterinaria*): Veterinary facility in a camp. *DMC* 4. [Johnson 1983]

vexillarius (m. pl. *vexillarii*): Standard-bearer who carried the *vexillum*. Liv. 8.8.4; Tac., *Hist.* 1.41.; *v. veteranorum CIL* V, 4903. See also *vexillifer* [Goldsworthy 2003]

vexillatio (f. pl. *vexillationes*): A detachment of troops mustered under a *vexillum* (Veg., *DRM* 2.1; Suet. *Galb.* 20); *v. comitatensis*: cavalry troops of the Late Roman mobile armies (*ND Oc.* 6; *Or.* 5); *v. palatina*: cavalry troops of the Late Roman mobile armies of higher rank than the *vexillationes comitatenses*, but not so high as the *scholae* (*ND Oc.* 6; *Or.* 5). [Goldsworthy 2003]

vexillifer (m. pl. *vexilliferi*): Standard-bearer who carried the *vexillum*. Prud., *Psych.* 419. See also *vexillarius* [Goldsworthy 2003]

vexillum (n. pl. *vexilla*): A square flag with a fringed lower edge suspended from a cross-bar. Used as a standard by a *vexillatio* and to give signals in the field. Caes., *BG* 6.36.3; *BC* 3.89; Veg., *DRM* 2.1. [Bishop and Coulston 2006] *via decumana* (f. pl. *viae decumanae*): Rear road into the fortress, passing through the *porta decumana*. In the *retentura*. *DMC* 18. [Johnson 1983]

via praetoria (f. pl. *viae praetoriae*): Main street running between the *porta praetoria* and the junction with the *via principalis*, directly in front of the *principia*. *DMC* 14. [Johnson 1983]

via principalis (f. pl. *viae principales*): Main street running between the *porta principalis sinistra* and *porta principalis dextra*. *DMC* 10. [Johnson 1983]

via quintana (f. pl. *viae quintanae*): Road parallel with the *via principalis* which formed a T-junction with the *via decumana*. Originally so-called because it divided the fifth and sixth *manipuli* and *turmae*. In legionary camps, this was not usually associated with *portae quintanae*. *DMC* 17. See also *quintana* [Johnson 1983]

via sagularis (f. pl. *viae sagularibus*). A road running around the periphery of the camp within the defences. Literally 'the cloaked street' (*DMC* 3). [Johnson 1983]

viaticum (n. pl. *viatica*): 1. An amount of money paid to an official to fund them to travel to their new province (Livy 44.22.13); 2. an amount of money paid to a new recruit to fund them to travel to their new unit, normally 75 *denarii* or 3 *aurei* (*RMR* 70). [Goldsworthy 2003]

via vicinaria (f. pl. *viae vicinariae*). A street between buildings, especially barracks. Literally 'local street'. *DMC* 13. [Johnson 1983]

vicanus (m. pl. *vicani*): Inhabitant of a *vicus*. *RIB* 1700; 3503. [Goldsworthy 2003]

victimarius (m. pl. *victimarii*): An individual who dealt with sacrifical animals at sacrifices. *CIL* VI, 2385; XIII,

Two **vexillarii** *with* **vexilla** *depicted on a metope from the* **Tropaeum Traiani**

8292. [Goldsworthy 2003]

vicus (m. pl. *vici*): A civil settlement outside a fort. *CIL* XI, 4748; XIII, 7335. [Johnson 1983]

vigil (m. pl. *vigiles*): 1. A guard or sentry (Caes., *BG* 8.35; Livy 44.33.8); 2. a member of the military watch and fire brigade in Rome, which was formed into seven cohorts under the Principate (Suet., *Aug.* 30.1). [Goldsworthy 2003]

vigilium (n. pl. *vigilia*): A night watch, each night being divided into four (the length of which depended upon the time of year and was monitored using a *clepsydra* or *horologium*). Veg., *DRM* 3.8; Livy 5.44.7. [Goldsworthy 2003]

vinea (f. pl. *vineae*): Literally a 'vine arbour', a wooden shed that formed part of a modular system for constructing covered walkways used by besiegers attacking a fortification. According to Vegetius, each was 8Rft (2.4m) wide, 16Rft (4.8m) long, and 7Rft (2.1m) high, with a roof covered in planking and sides in wattlework, an untanned leather or patchwork outer layer rendering the whole fireproof. Plaut., *Mil.* 2.2.113; Caes., *BG* 2.12.3; Veg., *DRM* 4.15. [Campbell 2003]

vitis (f. pl. *vites*). Carried as a badge of office by a *centurio* and made of vine wood. One man, Lucilius, famously breaking them whilst administering corporal punishment, was nicknamed 'Broke Another' (*cedo alteram*) according to Tacitus. Plin., *NH* 14.1.3; 19; Tac., *Ann.* 1.23; Luc. 6.146; Juv. 8.247. [Goldsworthy 2003]

xynema (Celt.): Part of the *hippika gymnasia* involving throwing javelins whilst changing course on horseback (Arr., *Tech. Tak.* 42). [Hyland 1993]

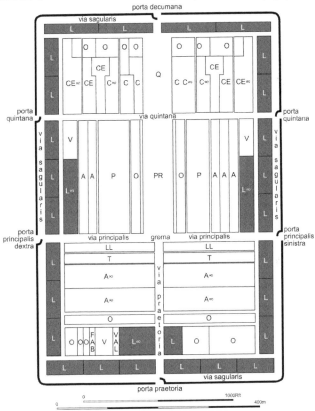

Temporary camp as described in the DMC. *Key:* L – *legionary* **cohors;** L∞ – *legionary* **cohors milliaria;** *P – Praetorian cohorts, cavalry, and* **equites singulares;** *A –* **ala** *of auxiliary cavalry;* A∞ – *double-strength* **ala milliaria;** *C –* **cohors** *of auxiliary infantry;* C∞ – **cohors milliaria** *of auxiliary infantry;* CE – **cohors equitata;** CE∞ – **cohors equitata milliaria;** O – *other;* LL – **scamnum legati;** T – **scamnum tribunorum;** VAL – **valetudinarium;** FAB – **fabrica;** Q – **quaestorium;** PR – **praetorium**

Appendix 1: Epigraphic abbreviations

Γ (*CIL* VIII, 2568–9; 18055–6) see *pilus posterior*

T (*CIL* VIII, 2568–9; 18055–6) see *princeps posterior*

⌐ (*AE* 2007, 1198) see *hastatus posterior*

⊥ (*AE* 2007, 1198) see *princeps prior*

⌐ (*AE* 2007, 1198) see *hastatus prior*

AL (*RIB* 586) see *ala*

AQ (*CIL* III, 11238) see *aquilifer*

AQVIL (*CIL* V, 3375) see *aquilifer*

ARM (*CIL* II, 864; VIII, 18320) see *armilla, armorum custos*

BF (*CIL* III, 14507) see *beneficiarius*

BF COS (*RIB* 725) see *beneficiarius consularis*

BF T (*CIL* III, 14507) see *beneficiarius tribuni*

BVC (*CIL* III, 3352) see *buccinator*

> (*RIB* 1573) see *centuria*

CA (*AE* 1908, 46; *CIL* XIII, 6996a) see *curam agens, custos armorum*

CAST (*CIL* VIII, 2586) see *castris*

CAST PRAET (*CIL* VI, 2772) see *castra praetoria*

CASTR (*CIL* VIII, 18084) see *castris*

CCC (*CIL* II, 4461) see *trecenarius*

CER (*CIL* III, 14507) see *cerarius*

CHO (*RIB* 121) see *cohors*

CL (*CIL* VI, 3092) see *classis*

COH (*RIB* 1288) see *cohors*

COR (*CIL* III, 14507) see *cornicularius*

CORNICVL (*CIL* III, 4405) see *cornicularius*

CP (*RIB* 1896) see *cui praeest*

CP EST (*RIB* 1893) see *cui praeest*

CV (*CIL* VIII, 2494) see *clarissimus vir*

CVR (*AE* 1984, 68) see *curator*

D (*CIL* VIII, 18086; *AE* 2003, 2058) see *discens, quingenaria*

DD (*CIL* III, 14507) see *donis donatus*

DS (*CIL* VIII, 2569) see *d. signifer(or)um*

DVPL (*CIL* III, 1067) see *duplarius, duplicarius*

EM (*RIB* 600) see *emeritus*

EME (*RIB* 3218) see *emeritus*

EQ (RIB 606; 1276) see *eques, equitata*

EVOC (*CIL* III, 14214,03b) see *evocatus*

GC (*CIL* XIII, 5966) see *genius castrorum*

HA POS (*AE* 1944, 28) see *hastatus posterior*

HAR (*CIL* III, 14214) see *haruspex*

HIB (*AE* 1938, 1) see *hiberna*

HM (*CIL* XVI, 69) see *honesta missio*

HON MIS (*AE* 1911, 97) see *honesta missione*

III (*CIL* XIV, 233) see *trieris*

IMAG (*CIL* III, 14214) see *imaginifer*

IMM (*CIL* VIII, 18084) see *immunis*

IMP (*RIB* 1638) see *imperator*

IS (*AE* 1992, 1458) see *sesquiplicarius*

KAS (*CIL* VIII, 18084) see *castris*

LATIC (*CIL* VIII, 18270) see *tribunus laticlavius*

LEG (*CIL* VIII, 18084, *RIB* 1638) see *legatus, legio*

LEG AVG PR PR (*RIB* 730) see *legatus Augusti pro praetore*

LEG LEG (*RIB* 658) see *legatus legionis*

LIB (*CIL* VIII, 2929) see *librarius*

∞ (*RIB* 1981) see *milliaria*

MIL (*RIB* 11; 1921; 1580) see *miles, militavit, milliaria*

NVM (*AE* 1962, 264) see *numerus*

OP (*CIL* VIII, 2482) see *optio*

OPT (*RIB* 809) see *optio*

ORD (*CIL* VI, 130) see *ordinarius, ordinatus*

PHAL (*CIL* VI, 1626) see *phalera*

PP (*RIB* 721; 502) see *praepositus, primus pilus*

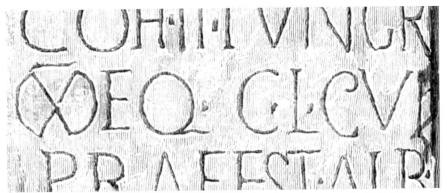

The symbol (centre left) for **milliaria** *on an altar from Castlesteads (*RIB *1981)*

PR (*RIB* 583) see *praefectus, princeps*

PRAEF (*RIB* 636) see *praefectus*

PRAEF CASTR (*RIB* 317) see *praefectus castrorum*

PRAEF LEG (*RIB* 326) see *praefectus legionis*

PRAEP (*RIB* 587) see *praepositus*

PR PR (*CIL* VI, 1009; III, 11135) see *praefectus praetorio, princeps prior*

PRI PRI (*CIL* VI, 3628) see *princeps prior*

QQ (*CIL* III, 7803) see *quaestionarius*

S (*CIL* VIII, 18086) see *signifer*

SAG (*CIL* XVI, 69; VIII, 2515) see *sagittaria, sagittarius*

SC (*RIB* 1266) see *singularis consularis*

SIG (*CIL* VIII, 18084) see *signifer*

SPECLAR (*AE* 2007, 1198) see *specularius*

STIP (*RIB* 121) see *stipendium*

STR (*CIL* III, 1675) see *strator*

T (*CIL* XIII, 6233; III, 5925; VI, 1057) see *testamentum, turma, tribunus*

TES (*CIL* III, 14214) see *tesserarius*

TORQ (*CIL* XI, 395) see *torques*

TRIB (*RIB* 1482) see *tribunus*

TVR (*RIB* 109) see *turma*

VET (*AE* 2002, 1237; *CIL* VI, 2772) see *veterana, veteranus*

VEX (*CIL* XIII, 11938; *RIB* 2205) see *vexillarius, vexillatio*

Appendix 2: Late Latin commands

A series of Latin commands has been preserved within the late 6th/early 7th century AD Greek text of the *Strategikon*, a military manual attributed to the Byzantine Emperor Maurikios (Maurice). Whether these are applicable to the Roman army is debatable, however, but many re-enactment groups have nevertheless used them as a basis for forming their own display scripts. Therefore, they are presented here for their curiosity value, if nothing else. References are to the most commonly available translation (Dennis 1984).

acia in acia: files in files (make formation 32 deep) 12.B.16.

ad conto clina move: to the right, face; march. 12.B.16.

ad decarchas: to the dekarchs.† 3.5.

ad fulcon: form the *fulkon*.* 12.B.16.

adiuta ...: help us... 12.B.16.

ad latus stringe: by the flank, close (close ranks). 3.3; 3.5.

ad octo: into eights (form up eight deep). 12.B.16.

ad pentarchas: to the pentarchs.† 3.5.

ad scuto clina move: to the left, face; march. 12.B.16.

bando‡ sequute: follow the standard. 12.B.14.

bandum capta: eyes on the standard. 3.5.

cede: give ground (fall back in open order). 3.5.

cum ordine seque: follow in order (with ranks closed). 3.5.

cursu mina: charge at a gallop. 3.5.

depone (ad) dextra: change front to the right. 3.5; 12.B.16.

depone (ad) senestra: change front to the left. 3.5; 12.B.16.

dirige frontem: dress rank. 12.B.16.

equaliter ambula: in line, march. 3.5.

exi: March out. 12.B.16.

intra: enter (increase formation depth). 12.B.16.

ipso seque cum bando milix: follow it (the standard) with your company, soldier. 3.5.

ipsum serve et tu bandifer: standard bearer, keep to your assigned position. 3.5.

iunge: close ranks. 3.4; 3.5; 12.B.16.

largia ad ambas partes: thin out the line (move to both sides). 12.B.16.

largiter ambula: open order, march. 3.2.

mandata captate: observe orders. 12.B.14.

medii partitis: divide in the middle. 12.B.16.

move: march. 3.5; 12.B.16.

muta locum: change places (front to rear) 12.B.16.

nemo antecedat bandum: do not advance in front of the standard. 3.5.

nemo demittat: do not fall back. 3.5.

nemo demittat bandum et inimicos seque: do not leave the standard and pursue the enemy. 12.B.14.

nobiscum (Deus): (God) be with us. 2.18.

non vos turbatis: do not worry. 12.B.14.

ordinem servate: hold position. 12.B.14.

parati: ready. 12.B.16.

percute: charge. 3.5.

primi state: first rank halt. 12.B.16.

redi: resume front. 12.B.16.

reverte: return. 12.B.16.

secundi ad difallangium exite: second rank march out, form double *phalanx*.* 12.B.16.

serva milix ordinem positum: soldier, keep your position. 3.5.

sic venias vero aequalis facies: advance even with the front rank. 3.5

silentium: silence. 3.5; 12.B.14.

sta: stand or halt. 3.5.

suscipe: first line falls back in second. 3.9.

talis est comodum miles barbate: this is how a brave soldier should act. 3.5.

torna mina: turn, threaten (wheel back). 3.5.

transforma: about face (turn in place) 3.5; 12.B.16.

transmuta: swap places (march to the back). 3.5.

undique servate: face in all directions. 12.B.16.

* Byzantine formation

† Byzantine officer

‡ Byzantine standard

Resources

The various sources cited here can nowadays be followed up online by a variety of means, ranging from databases to scanned copies of standard, out-of-copyright texts. These have revolutionised the way scholars work, and opened up even the most obscure primary sources to anybody who has access to the internet.

Lexicological

One of the most valuable online tools is **Lewis and Short's** *A Latin Dictionary*, available from the Perseus Digital Library at

http://tinyurl.com/LewisandShort

There is the odd transcription and/or scanning error, and not all of the hyperlinks to cited texts work properly, but feed them your corrections and they will improve it.

Literary

The **Perseus Digital Library** also has a comprehensive set of classical texts online, best browsed from

http://tinyurl.com/GreekandRomanTexts

but there is another good set (albeit without translations or notes) in **The Latin Library** at

http://www.thelatinlibrary.com

and that includes some missing from PDL (such as Vegetius and the *De Munitionibus Castrorum*). Even more obscure texts can usually be found as 19th century editions on **Archive.org** at

https://archive.org

Epigraphic

All of the inscriptions cited in this little book can be found on the (quite literally) monumental **Clauss-Slaby Epigraphic Database** at

http://tinyurl.com/Clauss-Slaby

This not only includes all of *CIL*, *ILS*, and *RIB*, but also more recent discoveries.

Sub-literary

The field of papyri, ostraca, and other sub-literary sources like writing tablets has not been left behind by technological developments either. Many papyri (including all of those in Fink 1971) can be accessed through **Papyri.info** on

http://papyri.info

whilst the **Vindolanda Writing Tablets** can be found at

http://tinyurl.com/TabVind

and many are also available from Clauss-Slaby (as are other writing tablets and some ostraca), once again on

http://tinyurl.com/Clauss-Slaby

Bibliography

Allen, W. S., *Vox Latina: A Guide to the Pronunciation of Classical Latin*, ed. 2, Cambridge

Bagnall, R. S., Helms, C. and Verhoogt, A. M. F. W. (2000): *Documents from Berenike. Volume 1, Greek Ostraka from the 1996–1998 Seasons*, Bruxelles

Bingen, J., Tomsin, A., Bodson, A., Denooz, J., Dupont, J. D. and Evrard, E. (1968): *Choix de papyrus grecs: Essai de traitement automatique*, Liège

Bishop, M. C. (2013): *Handbook to Roman Legionary Fortresses*, Barnsley

Bishop, M. C. (2014): *Ut Milites Dicuntur*, Per Lineam Valli **5**, Pewsey

Bishop, M. C. and Coulston, J. C. N. (2006): *Roman Military Equipment from the Punic Wars to the Fall of Rome*, ed.2, Oxford

Brand, C. E. (1968): *Roman Military Law*, Austin

Campbell, D. B. (2003): *Greek and Roman Siege Machinery 399 BC–AD 363*, New Vanguard **78**, Oxford

Cowan, R. (2007): *Roman Battle Tactics 109 BC–AD 313*, Elite **155**, Oxford

Cuvigny, H. (2012): *Didymoi: une garnison romaine dans le désert oriental d'Égypte. II, Les textes*, Paris

Dennis, G. T. (1984): *Maurice's Strategikon*, Philadelphia

Fink, R. O. (1971): *Roman Military Records on Papyrus*, Cleveland

Gilliam, J. F. (1967): 'The *deposita* of an auxiliary soldier. (P. Columbia inv. 325)', *Bonner Jahrbücher* 167, 233–43

Goldsworthy, A. (2003): *The Complete Roman Army*, London

Hyland, H. (1993): *Training the Roman Cavalry: from Arrian's Ars Tactica*, Stroud

Johnson, A. (1983): *Roman Forts of the 1st and 2nd Centuries AD in Britain and the German Provinces*, London

Jones, R. H. (2012): *Roman Camps in Britain*, Stroud

Keppie, L. J. (1984): *The Making of the Roman Army: from Republic to Empire*, London

Marichal, R. (1992): *Les Ostraca de Bu Njem*, Libya Antiqua, suppl. **9**, Tripoli

Maxfield, V. A. (1981): *The Military Decorations of the Roman Army*, London

Mynors, R. A. B. (1964), *XII Panegyrici Latini*, Oxford

Phang, S. E. (2001): *The Marriage of Roman Soldiers (13 BC–AD 235): Law and Family in the Imperial Army*, Leiden

Phang, S. E. (2008): *Roman Military Service: Ideologies of Discipline in the Late Republic and Early Principate*, Cambridge & New York

Salomons, R. P. (1996): *Papyri Bodleianae I*, Amsterdam

Southern, P. and Dixon, K. R. (1996): *The Late Roman Army*, London

Speidel, M. P. (1984): *Riding for Caesar: the Roman Emperors' Horse Guards*, London

Sumner, G. (2009): *Roman Military Dress*, Stroud

Watson, G. R. (1969): *The Roman Soldier*, London

Youtie, H. C. and Winter, J. G. (1951): *Michigan Papyri*, vol. 8, Ann Arbor

Topical indexes

Arms and equipment

arcus
arma
ballista
balteus
bracae
bucculla
buc(c)ina
caetra
calceus
caliga
capitulum
capulus
carroballista
cassis
catafracta
catapulta
cedo alteram
cento
cingulum militiae
clipeus
contus
cornu
crista
dolabra
draco
ephippium
falcata
falx
focale
framea
funda
fundibalus
furca
fustibalus
fustis
gaesum
galea
gladius

glans
groma
habitus
hasta
hastile
imago
impedimenta
insigne
lam(i)na
lancea
lorica
machaera
malleolus
manica
martiobarbulus
mattiobarbulus
monoxylus
murex
ocrea
onager
orarium
paenula
paludamentum
palus
papilio
parazonium
parma
patera
pectorale
pelta
persona
phalera
pil(l)eus
  Pannonicus
pilum
plumbata
pterygoma
pteryx
pugio
sagitta

sagum
scopa
scordiscus
scorpio
scutum
sella
semispatha
signum
spatha
stimulus
subarmalis
subpaenula
sudis
tabula ansata
tegimen
thoracomachus
tormentum
tribulus
trulla
tunica
umbo
vagina
vallus
vericulum
ver(r)utum
vexillum
vitis

Awards

armilla
armillata
bis armillata
bis torquata
civium Romanorum
corona
dona militaria
donativum
donis donatus
ob virtutem
  appellata

ornamenta
  triumphalia
phalera
torquata
torques

Battle

acies
ad signa convenire
ad triarios redisse
agmen
barritus
caput porci(num)
forceps
forfex
frons
globus
impedimenta
orbis
ordo
pugna publica
serra
signa convertere
subsidium
testudo
tropaeum

Conditions of Service

adlocutio
ad nomen
  respondere
aerorum
agentes in praesidio
agentes in rebus
albata decursio
buc(c)ellatum
calciarium
cibaria
classicum

clavarium
colonia
commeatus
depositum
diploma
domine
ex acuminibus
excubiae
faenaria
frater
frumentatio
frumentum
littera
  commendaticia
militavit
militia
mulus
muli Marlani
munifex
munus
opera vacantes
peregrinus
posca
praemia militiae
praesidium
probatio
quartum stipendium
sacramentum
salarium
salutatio militaris
Saturnalicium
seditio
sermo castrensis
spolia
statio
stationem agens
stipendiorum
stipendium
sub pellibus
sub vexillo
sub vineam iacare
sub vitem proeliari

tiro
tria nomina
vacatio munerum
veteranus
viaticum
vigilium

Fortification
aedes
 (principiorum)
aestivalia
agrimensor
amphitheatrum
aquaeductus
arma
armamentarium
ascensus
ballistarium
balneum
basilica
burgus
canabae
carcer
castellum
castra
castrum
cervus
cippus
clavicula
clepsydra
fabrica
forum
fossa
fossatum
hemistrigium
hiberna
hibernacula
horologium
horreum
intervallum
kastrum
latera praetorii

marching camp
mensor
metator
murus
noverca
officina
palus
papilio
per scamnum
per strigas
pinna
pons navalis
porta
praesidium
praetentura
praetorium
prata legionis
principia
propugnaculum
quaestorium
quincunx
quintana
retentura
sacellum
scamnum
 tribunorum
schola
striga
sudis
temporary camp
tentorium
titulum
tribunal
turris
valetudinarium
vallum
vallus
veterinarium
via decumana
via praetoria
via principalis
via quintana

via sagularis
via vicinaria
vicus

Legal
bona castrensia
castigatio
castrense peculium
causaria missio
causarius
cedo alteram
concessa
 consuetudo
coniunx
constitutio An-
 toniniana
conubium
decimatio
extra vallum tendere
focaria
fustuarium
honesta missio
ignominiosia missio
ius iurandum
matrimonium
militiae mutatio
missio
peculium castrense
pecuniaria multa
praeiuratio
praemia militiae
testamentum
transfuga

Naval
biremis
classis
cop(u)la
corvus
gubernator
harpago
liberna

manus
naupegus
nauta
pons navalis
rostrum
trierarchus
trieris

Organisation

accensus
acta militaria
aerarium militare
ala
antesignanus
aquila
areani
auxilia
Batavi
brevis
caetratus
centuria
cohors
comitatus
contubernium
corporis custodes
cui praeest
cuneus
dilectus
equitata
exercitus
foederatus
Germani corporis
  custodes
gradus
gravis armatura
hastatus
immunis
imperium
laetus
legio
levis armatura
limitaneus

magister
manipulus
matricula
mil(l)iaria
morning report
numerus
officium
ostraca
ostraka
pedites cohortales
postsignanus
pridianum
primus ordo
pseudocomitatensis
quingenaria
renuntium
ripensis
rorarius
schola
scutatus
socius
stator
sub cura
tabularium
tessera
tres militiae
  equestres
triarius
turma
veles
veterana
vexillatio
vigil

Ranks and Posts

act(u)arius
adiutor
aedituus
aerarius
antesignanus
aquilifer
arcanus

architectus
arcuarius
armicustos
armorum custos
asinarius
auxiliarius
ballistarius
beneficiarius
biarchus
bucellarius
buc(c)inator
caligatus
calo
capsarius
carcerarius
carpentarius
carrarius
castris
catafractarius
catafractus
cataphractarius
cataphractus
centenarius
centurio
cerarius
circitor
classiarius
clavicularius
clibanarius
cohortalis
comes
comitatensis
commentariensis
commilito
contarius
contubernalis
conturmalis
cornicen
cornicularius
curator
cursus honorum
custos armorum

decanus
decurio
discens
draconarius
dromedarius
ducenarius
duplarius
duplicarius
dux
eques
equis(i)o
evocatus
exactus
exceptor
explorator
faber
fabricensis
frumentarius
fundibalator
funditor
galearius
gladiarius
haruspex
horologiarius
imaginarius
imaginifer
immunis
imperator
interprex
lanciarius
legatus Augusti pro
  praetore
legatus (Augusti)
  legionis
legionarius
librarius
librator
lictor
medicus
mensor
metator
miles

munifex
officialis
optio
ordinatus
ordo
pecuarius/pequarius
phalangarius
pilus
praefectus
praepositus
praesentalis
praesidiarius
praetorianus
primus pilus
princeps
principalis
quaestionarius
quaestor
quintanensis
sacerdos
sagittarius
scutarius
secutor
semissalis
sesquiplarius
sesquiplicarius

signifer
singularis
specularius
speculator
stator
strator
subpraefectus
supernumerarius
symmach(i)arius
tesserarius
trecenarius
tribunus
veteranus
veterinarius
vexillarius
vexillifer
vicanus
victimarius
vigil

Religion
armilustrium
dies natalis aquilae
disciplina
Feriale Duranum
genius

haruspex
honori aquilae
iovis
lustratio
natalis aquilae
omnia vos
optime maxime …
rosaliae signorum
Saturnalicium
utere felix

Siege warfare
agger
aries
ballista
catapulta
cippus
circumvallatus
exostra
harpago
lillia
lupus
manus
musculus
onager
pluteus

sambuca
scala
stimulus
sub vineam iacare
sub vitem proeliari
testudo
tolleno
tormentum
vinea

Training
ambulatum
ambulatura
armatura
campestres
campicursio
campidoctor
campus
decursio
disciplina
exercitatio
exercitator
gradus
hippika gymnasia

More information about Hadrian's Wall is available online at **perlineamvalli.org.uk**

Read the Per Lineam Valli blog at
perlineamvalli.wordpress.com

Follow **@perlineamvalli** on Twitter at
twitter.com/perlineamvalli

This book is also available from *Amazon* for Kindle

M. C. Bishop is a freelance writer, publisher, and archaeologist who walks, drives, cycles, flies, tweets, blogs, draws, and photographs Hadrian's Wall armed only with a Creative Commons licence. He is the author of *Lorica Segmentata Vol. 1*; *Corstopitum: An Edwardian Excavation*; numerous dull excavation reports; and co-author (with J. C. N. Coulston) of *Roman Military Equipment* and (with J. N. Dore) *Corbridge: Excavations of the Roman Fort and Town 1947–1980* (neither of which are at all dull). When he grows up he will definitely get a real job.

The **centurio** *Facilis from Colchester-Camulodunum, with a* **balteus, gladius, pugio, vitis, lorica, pteryges, ocreae,** *and* **paludamentum,** *also illustrating the use of the >* *and* **LEG** *abbreviations in his memorial inscription.*

Printed in Great Britain
by Amazon